Can't
Help
Falling

.II.

Can't Help Falling

A LONG ROAD TO MOTHERHOOD

a memoir

TARAH SCHWARTZ

Prepared for the press by Elise Moser
Copyedited and proofed by Deanna Radford and Edward He
Author photo by Hera Bell
Cover design by Leila Marshy
Graphic design by Debbie Geltner
Cover image iStock DNY59
Book design by DiTech Publishing Services, India.

Library and Archives Canada Cataloguing in Publication

Title: Can't help falling : a long road to motherhood : a memoir / Tarah Schwartz.
Names: Schwartz, Tarah, author.
Identifiers: Canadiana (print) 20210335939 |
Canadiana (ebook) 20210335947 | ISBN 9781773901084 (softcover) |
ISBN 9781773901091 (EPUB) | ISBN 9781773901107 (PDF)
Subjects: LCSH: Schwartz, Tarah. | LCSH: Miscarriage—Psychological aspects. |
LCSH: Parental grief—Canada. | LCSH: Mothers—Canada—Biography. |
LCSH: Motherhood—Canada. | LCSH: Television journalists—Canada—
Biography. | LCGFT: Autobiographies.
Classification: LCC RG648 .S39 2022 | DDC 613.3/92092—dc23

Printed and bound in Canada.

The publisher gratefully acknowledges the support of the Government of Canada through the Canada Council for the Arts, the Canada Book Fund, and of the Government of Quebec through the Société de développement des entreprises culturelles (SODEC).

Linda Leith Publishing
Montreal
www.lindaleith.com

For my two great loves, Enrico and Sam.

The truest, most beautiful life never promises to be an easy one. We need to let go of the lie that it's supposed to be.

— Glennon Doyle, *Untamed*

You have to keep breaking your heart until it opens.

— Rumi

Table of Contents

Faith 91

Family   114

Epilogue   174

Sorrow

1 What We Can Survive

I knew my life would never be the same. The feeling was powerful. It pulled me apart at the seams and when I glued myself back together, the pieces were skewed and misaligned. The baby that had lived inside me for almost five months passed away. One moment his tiny heart was beating, and the next, that gentle pulsing ceased to exist. It wasn't just my son that I mourned, but an entire life I had built up inside my head. I had to bury that as well.

I had been taught that nothing was beyond my reach, I simply had to work for it, fight for it if necessary. But somehow, getting pregnant and having a child refused to come easy. It refused to come at all. It instilled in me a feeling of helplessness. That's how I felt about becoming a mother. Helpless.

Like so many others, I wanted to live through the wonder of pregnancy. I wanted to experience unconditional love. This desire felt like a knowing; the deep-down belief that some unnamed part of me was meant to do this. But that dream came at a cost. It changed who I was and pushed me down unwelcome and unwanted roads. Before I finally became a mother, I faced challenges I wasn't sure I could survive.

I first became pregnant just after my 38th birthday. The months passed and my belly grew. I heard my child's heartbeat and felt him kick and move. It was a very long way to fall from the clouds I was walking on, to the bed I refused to get out of once the being who shared my body was no longer there. The agony is indescribable. That miscarriage led to several others. I could get pregnant, but was unable to sustain pregnancy for more than a few months. For many years, I navigated sorrow after sorrow.

Miscarriages are not often talked about openly in our society, and parents mourn alone, unsure of how to share their sadness about something that no one else saw or felt.

I'm sharing my story about the moments that led me from being lost to finding the kind of love I knew I wanted. I don't want to imply that there are always happy endings, but they do exist.

I hope this story helps cultivate empathy for all that loss. I hope it will foster understanding for those who don't know how to offer comfort. And I hope it will offer grace to every woman who has ever cried herself to sleep. I am with you.

2 Beloved

I met my husband on Friday the 13th in the bleakest, coldest month of the year. In spite of the superstition usually associated with that day and date, our relationship began with one look that led to years of love. Enrico is tall with brown hair and has eyes the colour of moss, a woody green with flecks of gold at the edges. On our second date I arrived at the restaurant to find a long-stemmed red rose at my place setting. My husband is an old soul who believes in romantic gestures. Fourteen years later, he still leaves sweet notes stuck to mirrors in our home, and my pulse still quickens when I catch a glimpse of one of them.

Enrico has a wise quality about him. He's loyal and protective, walking on the side of traffic or picking me up at work if I finish late. He makes me laugh, and he thinks I'm hilarious. Early on in our relationship, problems that came up didn't always get resolved right away, but learning to communicate calmly is one of many lessons I have learned from him.

"I need time to think about what you said," he would say. "And then we can talk."

There was no distress in his voice, no sense of menace. No worry that our entire relationship would implode if we didn't resolve a problem at that very moment.

"It's alright," he'd say. "I just want to think about it, really think about it, and then we'll figure it out."

That kind of problem-solving was new to me. My instinct was to throw every issue onto the table then frantically dig for answers through the chaos, searching for solutions I could barely recognize. Eventually, I learned that time could be a gift. Giving Enrico the time he needed got easier, and I came to see that taking an hour or a day to think things through was good for me too.

We married in the fall, and by spring I was pregnant. Spring in Montreal is magical. The sky transforms from the deep blue of peacock feathers in the bitter cold of winter, to a paler shade the colour of pool water. Snow melts, rain washes down, puddles filled with ash-coloured water dry out. Birds start singing and buds sprout on thin branches of trees that are as hunched and tired as old men. Street cleaners busily sweep up months of dirt, flowers poke through sodden earth, and dry grass stands at attention. The heat prompts people to shed the warm layers that have held them captive all winter long, their wool and fleece clothes replaced by cotton in colours with names like tangerine and melon.

When I became pregnant, I was ecstatic. I was relieved, too, as I had been told by my doctor that closing in on 40 would make it more difficult to conceive. OK, I told myself when I found out, I didn't wait too long, I didn't miss my chance.

Like many women, I had been holding off for the right time to start a family—the right person, the right job milestone. I wanted first to travel and do all the things that having a baby might change, including sleeping, binge-watching TV shows during the day, or leaving for a weekend away at a moment's notice. But time caught up with me. As I stared at the positive pregnancy test, bought when I was ever-so-slightly late, I felt incredibly grateful. I ran down the stairs of our home into my husband's arms and told him we were going to be parents. We laughed nervously and held each other close.

I continued a regular yoga practice, endeavouring to live every moment aware and awake. I lay on my mat and passed mostly unscathed through early days that were filled with nausea and fatigue. I documented every millimetre of my growing belly with an almost ridiculous devotion. My favourite teacher, Antoine, often began his classes with lessons about living in the moment, reminding us that there could be no happiness without sadness, no light without dark, no day without night—that it is impossible to fully know one without the other.

"The tighter we hold on to something," Antoine cautioned, "the more challenging it is to let it go."

I sat and listened, hearing him, but perhaps not fully understanding. I was so happy but ironically, I was holding onto it so very tightly. There was a sublime future drawn and coloured inside my head that included this baby. I was convinced there was no other possibility.

As the months passed, the extraordinary moments continued. My body expanded to allow room for another person, a first kick alerted me that someone inside of me was stretching, that a foot or an elbow was seeking space. I held Enrico's hand over my growing belly.

"It's incredible," he said.

"It truly is. I can feel a little human inside me, one that we created."

My doctor advised me to have an amniocentesis, a test recommended for women over thirty-five that detects health issues with the baby.

"There is some risk," Dr. Samson explained.

"What kind of risk?" I asked. "And how risky is risky?"

"The needle used to draw out the amniotic fluid could nick the baby or cause an infection. The chances are minimal, but they exist. It's your choice, but I think it's a good idea."

I was sure she wanted to add *at your age* at the end of her sentence, but she didn't.

"Alright," I agreed. "I guess it's better to know if there's a problem. But there won't be."

"I'm sure you're right," Dr. Samson said.

Even as I went through the procedure, which was far less painful and scary than I had imagined, I didn't believe anything would go wrong. Enrico and I had a chance to see the baby through a powerful ultrasound monitor. It was curled up and sleeping inside me. We saw the tip of the needle pierce my uterus and watched as the line it represented moved closer to the sac in which our child was nestled.

"You can see how far the baby is from the needle," said the technician. "That's good. He's not moving, which is exactly what we want."

"He?" We both asked.

"Oh, I'm so sorry!" she said. "I can't tell for sure, but I think so."

I couldn't believe it. It was a boy.

Enrico squeezed my hand. "A boy," he whispered. Our gazes stayed connected.

Once the needle was removed and the precious liquid collected, we were allowed to hear his heartbeat.

"It's strong," she said. "A perfect, steady beat." We stayed quiet, listening to the distant drumming. I was just over four months pregnant.

The nausea had passed, my energy was back, and when a dear friend invited me to Toronto for a long hot summer weekend, I eagerly agreed.

"It will be good for you," Enrico said. "D'Arcy has a boat, doesn't he?"

"Oh yes, he does!"

D'Arcy and I had been roommates during our university years, and he kept a boat moored on Toronto Island. I left Montreal looking forward to a catch-up near the water. We spent long days eating, swimming, walking, and reading. In the evenings, we returned to his condo to decide on dinner and a movie before I fell asleep on his couch.

On the third day of my trip, my thoughts were carefree and my body even more relaxed than before—yoga lessons put to good use—Enrico called.

"Hi sweetheart," I said, happy to hear his voice.

We talked about nothing important: what he had for dinner, how his day was at work, something funny our cats did, and when I would be home. "Soon," I said. "I'll be home soon."

"Oh, I almost forgot," he said as we were about to say goodbye. "Dr. Samson left a message on the house machine. She's been trying to contact you and wants you to call her as soon as you can."

I felt sick instantly. "When did she leave the message?" I asked. "Why didn't you tell me sooner? What did she say?"

Enrico saw no cause for concern. "It just sounded like the kind of message a doctor would leave," he said. "Just call her tomorrow, I'm sure everything is fine."

"Something is wrong. Something has to be wrong. Why else would she call?"

For the first time in a long time, my happiness gave way to something else: fear. I couldn't slow it down or fight it off. It was caught far down in my throat, refusing to move, making it hard to speak or swallow. Both Enrico and D'Arcy kept telling me the same thing, not to worry. What they failed to understand was the impossibility of what they were asking. Despite my yoga and meditation practice, I was failing miserably at staying calm. I was miles away watching my precious future crumble like dried flower petals. I knew there was nothing I could do until the next day. I also knew it was going to be a very long night.

"Try not to imagine the worst," D'Arcy urged. What else was there to say?

The night taunted me with its stillness and solitude. The numbers on the clock inched forward as I watched a full moon track across the sky. At 7 a.m., with bleary-eyes and nervous energy making my body twitch, I began calling the doctor's office. Every five minutes I punched in the numbers, letting it ring before hanging up and then dialling again.

"The doctor isn't here yet, Tarah," the secretary said when she finally picked up the phone. "I'll get her to call you when she arrives."

My voice was dry as a desert while my eyes overflowed. I begged her to tell me what was in my file. She resisted, but I was relentless. Eventually she offered one ever so tiny word that shattered me into thousands of pieces.

"Just tell me, is there something wrong with the baby?" I begged.

I heard her take a breath. I held mine.

"Yes."

"Is it bad?"

"Yes."

3 The Inescapable Truth

I collapsed. I screamed louder than anything I had ever heard come out of my mouth. I was terrified. The suffering was so intense it cut through my body like razors. It unleashed a fury so quick and powerful I did not think my body could bear it. The violent emotions made me feel as if I was being ripped apart. I couldn't breathe, couldn't move, couldn't function, couldn't cope. So I cried. I just cried and cried and cried.

I'm not sure how long I lay on the floor. Long enough to feel the cool concrete seep into my cheek, leaving it ice cold. I remember thinking that I had to get up. Just get up.

D'Arcy had left early for a few hours of work, so I was alone with the most tragic news I had ever received. I stood there trying to pull myself together. Toronto is a five-hour drive from Montreal or a one-hour plane ride. Digging into some sunken place within myself, I foraged for a way to get through the next few hours.

I made phone calls. To Enrico first. To tell him I was coming home. That I loved him. To say the words that felt unendurable as they passed through my lips.

"The baby isn't well," I told him, barely able to breathe.

"Tell me," he said.

My husband is a quiet man. He listens more than he speaks. There were long moments of silence where he said nothing while I wept.

"We'll get through this," Enrico said, his voice thin and strained. "Come home."

I called the airline.

Packed my clothes.

Took a taxi to the airport.

Boarded a plane.

I sat by the window and watched heart-shaped clouds break into pieces as the jet's wings sliced through them. Throughout the trip I fought an almost unbearable desire to sob. The power of my pain threatened to consume me, and I was able to function only by waging war against it. It took a shocking amount of energy. It felt, quite literally, like I was holding myself together.

Enrico was at the airport. He wrapped his arms around me and held my body to his. I could not speak, not a single word. What was there to say?

We were silent as we drove to Dr. Samson's office. Sitting before her, separated by a desk and a million miles, the disconnect between us as a couple and the rest of the world began. I could see Dr. Samson's mouth moving, but I couldn't hear anything she said. She seemed so far away, her white lab coat getting dimmer with each sentence.

"I know this is terrible news," she said, sympathetically.

We said nothing.

"It's important that we make plans," she continued. "Your pregnancy is already very far along; we need to act quickly."

I stared beyond her at a cream-coloured wall, my eyes fixed on its drabness with an intensity that I needed to keep me from disappearing completely.

I forced myself to speak. "Is there anything we can do?"

"I'm sorry," she said.

The hold I had on myself gave way again. Unable to accept what she was saying, I started heaving. There was no escape from her words. There was nowhere to hide from the truth, because the truth was inside me. It was the most devastating moment of my life.

"I'll make the call," Dr. Samson said, and then she left the room.

I felt barely conscious in the following days, only a fragile shadow who managed to talk with family, sign papers, and lie in bed with the curtains closed. Part of me slipped away during those days, washed down a bottomless drain never to be seen or heard from.

My father held my hand as we chose an urn and made arrangements for the cremation. I saw his strong shoulders slump under a weight even he could not carry or will away.

Less than a week later, I lay in a hospital bed. A kind doctor let me stare at the ultrasound of our child for as long as I needed. I cried the entire time, willing this wretched moment to be a dream I could wake up from. I remember the doctor had white hair and limpid blue eyes, fatherly even in his appearance. He touched my cheek, a gesture filled with immeasurable kindness, as he said he was going to sedate me. I lost consciousness, watching the room fade away. Then that gentle doctor took my son out of my body.

The months afterwards were airless and suffocating. Our lives became an old black-and-white movie, something colourless we watched rather than lived. Flashes of what might have been dropped before our eyes like birds falling from the branch of a tree.

There are no words to convey the heartbreak, one can only describe the breaking. For days after the procedure I stared at the sky and searched for... I'm not sure what. God? Some comfort that I could not find anywhere on Earth. I never wanted to die, but I desperately wanted to stop existing. At least for a short while. I wanted to close my eyes and wake up in the future, some place far away.

4 Katie

I have spent much of my life telling stories and asking questions. As a former broadcast journalist for the CTV Television Network in Montreal, telling stories was part of the job description. It is a privilege to witness profound moments in people's lives: to see hurts and hopes up close, how anguish or triumph can imprint a soul, and the way fossils bury into stone deeply over time. Some stories humbled me and helped me to become a better person. Others evoked such tenderness. There are faces of people I've interviewed that even after many long years, I can still see clearly. Katie's face is one of them.

On assignment for CTV, I boarded a plane with only two dozen seats and far too much turbulence. We were heading toward northern Quebec where, in the middle of winter, temperatures dip easily to minus 40 degrees celsius. I was to write and produce a half-hour report on a unique expedition to follow a dozen young cancer patients over ten days. Led by a Quebec foundation called On the Tip of the Toes, its mission was to take sick teenagers who could travel without their parents, out of a hospital environment, immerse them in nature, and help them to see how strong they really are.

"You don't like to fly, do you?" one of the teenagers from Toronto asked as I gripped the handles of my seat. She said her name was Katie.

"No," I laughed. "I really don't. Tell me, how are you staying so calm?"

"I don't worry about the plane crashing," she explained. "It seems silly to worry about something you have no control over."

"That's a good point," I said. "I'll try to remember that. Once the plane gets back on the ground."

We landed late morning in the Cree village of Waskaganish where wide, white landscapes stretched in every direction beyond an invisible horizon line. We bundled our bodies under layers of down, our breath puffing out in long ghostlike wisps that shuddered in place for a moment before drifting skyward. We checked into a beautiful lodge built of sturdy wood that had carpeted floors and a blazing fire at the centre of a circular lounge. The daylight faded quickly and, away from windows and doors where light spilled out in yellow pools, the sky was so intensely black and vast it threatened to swallow you whole. When they arrived, the Northern Lights swept in with bright greens and blazing pinks that dusted the sky with colourful jewels. You can only see these collisions between electrically charged particles above the magnetic poles in the northern and southern hemispheres. That's how far from home we had come.

"How will you get them to talk to you?" asked Robert, our cameraman.

"We wait," I said. "They'll come when they're ready. And we have the luxury of time."

It's hard to imagine the challenges these teenagers were coping with—what young person should ever have to contemplate death? Katie was fifteen years old and had an aggressive form of soft-tissue cancer. Her prognosis was uncertain. She didn't immediately open up, but for two days I felt her watching me.

"If you'd like to talk to me, that would be OK," she finally said. "I guess my story is worth telling."

"I would very much like to hear it," I told her. "I have no doubt you have something very special to share."

As it happened, Katie and I were snowmobiling partners, which forges something precious in that kind of cold. Led by Victor, our Cree guide, our group of around 20 which included Quebec nature guides, a doctor and a child psychologist, began our journey snowmobiling across the bottom of James Bay. We sat together on long rides, pulled together for warmth, and from that sheltered place grew moments of closeness.

"I don't like to think about *what if*," she said once.

"Are you glad you're here?" I asked her. "Do you think it will help?"

"I am glad I'm on this trip. If I can't beat the cancer, this is one more life experience. And I want to have as many of those as possible." She seemed inexplicably serene. She was hard and soft all at once.

"I'm really glad to be away from home for a bit," she added. "The change of scenery is welcome."

It may seem strange, bringing sick kids into seemingly harsh terrain, but I tell you, there is healing there. For two weeks, they were so much more than just kids with cancer dealing with hospital appointments and invasive tests; they were part of a group that was doing something adventurous and unique. And because they all had the same illness, they shared a quiet understanding of each other's path and burdens.

We stopped and camped in small villages that seemed to pop up out of nowhere, listened to elders recite stories of hope and perseverance after feasting on meat such as seal and caribou that many of us had never tried before. Victor gifted us a sunset visit to a sweat lodge, where the women of our group slipped into the warmth in our underwear.

"This is a sacred place," Victor explained. He had a kind smile and a thick head of brown hair that he pulled back in a ponytail.

"Let the heat help you heal," he encouraged. "Look inward and find what makes you, you."

Victor taught us how the Inuit hunted, what they believed in, how they watched and respected the land.

"The land," he explained, "is alive."

I believe that in those days they felt an incredible strength and a power they didn't realize they had. I believe they felt very much alive.

"It's also a relief to be away from the hospital," Katie told me. "It's so heavy there, and despite everyone's best efforts at being positive, I get it. I get that I might die."

"That sounds scary," I said. "How do you manage that?"

"I guess I just live. I don't think there's anything else I can do."

When I say it's a privilege to witness intimate moments, those words at that moment are what I mean. She was just a child, one with such an unfair burden. Robert and I documented as much of that living as we could, which in those ten days consisted of travelling and witnessing. Crossing that frozen tundra, I imagined our small group under the glass of a snow globe unaware that we had been flipped over, and then flipped back again, so silent strangers could watch us as we moved.

At each stop we learned more about the blessings of life and the inevitability of death. We were encouraged by those who lived by the shores of James Bay to embrace the silence that lives in the north. Victor, who loved to laugh and share, never passed up an opportunity to impart a lesson. He knocked on our cabin doors very late one night and pulled us from our beds.

"Let's experience the dark and the silence together," he whispered. Every one of us followed him into the night.

Down on our knees, eyes closed, our breath the only trace of a whisper on the wind, I realized that if this was silence I had never heard it before. It was as if the universe was holding its breath and we were caught in the hush, right before an exhalation.

"Do you hear that?" Katie whispered to me as we sat side by side in the snow. She slipped her mittened hand in mine.

"I want to yell that it's unfair," Katie explained during one of our many interviews, "but I won't." The chemotherapy had left her with no hair, eyelashes or eyebrows, but she was beautiful.

"You always seem very strong, what is it like when you're not?"

"I don't think it's strength," she said. "I think it's powerlessness. I have a wonderful family and great friends and great doctors, but in the end, I have no control over my life."

I kept my eyes on hers. I gave her space to continue.

"I wish so many things were different." Katie went on. "I wish I knew that I would grow up, that I would live. I have a lot to do, you know."

"I can see that. And I want you to do it all. I really do."

Katie looked at me for a while without saying another word. Then her blue eyes, the colour of the ocean, grew watery and greyer, and her tears tipped over her lids, and crawled down her face. I wrapped my arms around her, her head resting on my shoulder, and in those few quiet moments, I felt some infinitesimal part of her bury itself in me. I think that's why I have always remembered her. I'm sure Robert does as well, for in that melancholic moment he did something I have rarely seen in the TV business. He chose compassion over compelling visuals. He turned off his camera, allowed Katie her privacy, and walked away.

Katie did die. Two years after we met, I flew to her bedside to say goodbye. She was frail and incredibly thin. Her eyes never opened, not once, but she whispered a little. I held her hand, so cold and pale. Her skin was translucent, as if most of the life had already drained from her body. As I sat by her, strange as this may seem, I sang a lullaby.

Katie's mother was a woman of compassion. I had met her only once before, on the day we landed after our expedition and our group parted ways. Then in the hospital, where we hugged in silence for several minutes. The death of her daughter was so heavy she could barely stand. Katie was her only child, and in her face I witnessed pure, impenetrable grief.

It was a look I never forgot.

5 The Little Boys of Christmas

In the days after we lost the baby, I woke up every morning only to begin counting the hours until I could go back to bed. The days were eternal. My chest was in a constant state of contraction, with pressure like a nail being pushed slowly but steadily through something soft.

Enrico and I barely spoke. I think we both knew that if we opened our mouths we would risk emptying ourselves of whatever we had left. Grief moved into our house, where it took up space—more than I expected, and more than we had to give.

We watched how life around us seemed to just go on while our lives had stopped. It seemed unimaginable that the earth did not get tangled in our turmoil and stop spinning.

Most people don't know what to do or say. They stumble over uncomfortable silences, trip on strands of misplaced words. The awkwardness sends them tiptoeing in the opposite direction, returning only when the rough edges have been smoothed out. That can be too late. Grief tears at the connection between people, fraying it.

"I'm going back to work," I told Enrico.

"It's only been two weeks. Are you sure you're ready?"

"Probably not, but I'm going anyway."

I needed to be back in a busy newsroom. I needed distance and distraction from endless reminders. My days were being spent packing up boxes, organizing closets, relentlessly cleaning, and sleeping. There were not enough activities in my home to consume me. In a television station the opportunities for escape are limitless.

Those first days back, I was conscious of heads turning to look at me with a mix of discomfort and sympathy. Kind words were offered, to which I nodded politely. An older colleague stepped over to my desk and, without a word, kissed the top of my head then walked away.

September passed. So did October.

Then November.

And December.

I wanted to feel better, but healing only happens gradually, in thin layers. I wanted to smile or laugh, but that was elusive, like something I only remembered doing. I wanted to be pregnant again, but that didn't happen either. And with each passing month, as no new life took hold inside me, hope bled away.

To those around me, it must have seemed like I had moved on. That's what happens, after all. People move on, don't they? As the holidays approached, reporters were assigned Christmas features to help fill a news lull toward the end of December. Mine was the story of a family who had six boys, all under the age of six. Six boys under the age of six!

Great, I said to myself, wondering how on earth I would get through the day, unsure the armour I had been building was strong enough to survive it. *Let's get this over with.*

An evergreen tree covered in bright holiday bulbs stood at attention before their home. The cameraman and I were greeted by a couple and three of their sons, ages six, four and two. Six-month-old triplets slept quietly nearby. The children welcomed us into their ebullient world full of toys, food, clutter, and conversation. We filmed their Christmas chaos, a story meant to bring holiday cheer. I kept reminding myself to breathe.

The eldest boy never strayed far from my side. He wore glasses, had a mop of blond hair that fell onto his face, and he watched me intensely with incredibly large eyes. He had so many things he wanted to tell me.

Chatty children are a reporter's dream. They are honest, impulsive and hold nothing back. He told me how his younger brother wouldn't leave his things alone, that finding his own private space was important, yet all too often impossible. He discussed his baby brothers and how the dinner table was too crowded. He explained with utter seriousness, what toys worked best and which ones his brothers had damaged beyond repair. Before I knew it, I was smiling.

When I asked what he wanted for Christmas that year, he paused to think about a question that, at six, clearly needed careful consideration. I can't remember what he asked for. What I do remember is what he did next.

Deciding he wanted to ask the questions, he took my microphone and pointed it at me.

"What do you want for Christmas?" he asked.

I didn't answer at first. This home was so full of joy that I had been infected by it. And joy was something I hadn't felt in quite a while. That question risked opening wounds that were only gently hidden over. He asked again, "What do you want, Miss Tarah?"

His eyes were so curious and full of wonder, and he barely blinked. Patiently he waited, so I answered him, as honestly as I could.

"I want a little boy just like you."

6 A Barren Land

I wanted so badly to become pregnant again. We tried for a year. And then for a few more months after that. People told us to relax, that it would happen. I'm telling you right now, never say that to people trying to have a baby. It doesn't help, not even a bit. It diminishes the struggle, reduces it to something far too simple.

Enrico and I wanted the process of conceiving a child to be loving, but it began to feel like a mountain we struggled to climb, the peak seeming farther and farther away, no matter how many steps we took. It was exhausting.

"What if I can never carry a child to term?"

"Then we won't have children, and that will be OK."

"It won't be," I said. "I feel guilty, like I'm failing you. You want to be a father. What if I can't give that to you?"

Enrico pulled me into his arms. "I need you to hear this," he said. "This is not your fault. You give me everything."

"Not a baby."

"I would rather spend my life with you without children," Enrico said, "than have children with someone else."

It was hard to hear that. And even harder to believe it. I didn't want to imagine our lives without a child. Not yet. It felt too soon to give up. That's when we decided to enter the world of In Vitro Fertilization.

"Are you sure you want to do this?" Enrico asked.

"I want to at least try."

"Then we'll try." Again, with him, it was few words. "I love you."

Over a period of about eighteen months, I underwent IVF three times. Every conceivable test showed us to be completely healthy, but I was forty. And while I had some idea of how age can affect fertility, I had no idea how significantly. There are certainly exceptions, but the majority of women who seek help conceiving are over thirty-five years old. It makes sense; our eggs decrease in quantity and are less robust the older we get.

Each session of IVF takes about two months. It involves multiple hospital visits and, at the beginning, daily injections of hormones. The goal is to stimulate egg growth, eggs that will eventually be retrieved from the body, fertilized in a lab, and then returned to the womb where they will grow.

It's not an easy process. The hormones are stimulants that increase in strength each day. With every injection, I felt as though a swollen, heavier version of myself had moved inside my body, making it far too crowded.

I kept my infertility secret, too embarrassed and too ashamed to admit I was undergoing treatment. After early morning hospital visits where doctors evaluated my progress, I went straight into work. I took deep breaths, reminded myself why I was doing this, and pulled open the doors to the busy newsroom.

Things move quickly in the news business. The job demands clarity, an ability to think quickly, synthesize information, and speak on live television composed and self-assured with often minimal time to prepare. It's not as easy as it looks, but also rarely as hard as it was during this period.

During that first treatment cycle, I was assigned a story about the death of a young woman who had passed away during, of all things, a standard nose job. A press conference was held by Quebec's most well-known medical malpractice lawyer, and there was no question it would have full media coverage—dozens of reporters, photographers, writers, and camera people all in one too-small room. The press conference was set to begin at 10:30 a.m., and my cameraman and I were late, arriving just as the lawyer was getting up to leave the table. My hormone-riddled self, pumped and pushing at me from the inside, walked right up to the lawyer as cameras were clicking and videos were filming. I heard a communal groan from my colleagues, who were ready to pack up and file their stories. As the adrenaline kicked in, I knew it was going to be a very long day.

Less than an hour later, I reported live with our news anchor, forcing my mind to stay clear and focused as I explained the nature of the lawsuit and the tragic way the young woman had died. It felt like forever until I heard the producer's voice in my ear saying, "You're clear!" I exhaled, walked back into the bathroom of the lawyer's office, and held my head in my hands. The struggle against the effects of the drugs was gruelling.

I continued with my regular yoga practice, often staying after class to find comfort in the words of my teacher Antoine. "Give the hormones the room they need," he encouraged. "They are there anyways. You might as well welcome them."

Antoine wanted me to become familiar with the drugs so that we could coexist without acrimony. His teachings always brought me back to reality, to sit quietly, and to accept what was.

"I don't feel like myself," I explained. "It's uncomfortable and scary. I don't recognize myself."

"If you fight this process Tarah, it will fight you back," he said. "Try acceptance and see what happens."

"You make it sound so simple."

"Maybe it could be," he said. "It's completely up to you. You are going through the procedure, and still you have no control."

Letting go of control has been a lifelong challenge, and I think I'm far from alone in that regard. Realizing that no matter how much we try to script our lives, make it perfect, and choose wisely, life will include both joyous moments and horrible ones that cannot be planned for. We can make choices and anticipate certain outcomes, but we cannot know what the future holds.

At the end of the first round of IVF I took the much-anticipated pregnancy test. It came back negative.

"I'm sorry," was all our doctor could say. Dr. Holzer was a leading IVF specialist. His strong Israeli accent reminded me of my father's.

"I know it's disappointing," said Dr. Holzer. "But it is only a first try. Many women have to try more than once."

The words dropped from his mouth hot as coal, so hot I could swear the room smelled like burnt wood. How could my pregnancy test be negative when we did everything right? A healthy embryo was implanted inside me. I could not understand why it did not live.

There are no answers to those questions, no satisfactory explanations of any kind, nothing that soothes. Only words that scrape as painfully as sandpaper. It simply did not work, was what our doctor said and somehow, that had to be enough.

"We'll try again," he said kindly. "We'll try again and get better results. You must not give up."

We sat in his office, feeling defeated, and agreed to try again. There was no other option that seemed less awful.

The second round of IVF was easier. Instead of walking through an impenetrable gloom, it was more like crawling through a dimly lit tunnel while sweeping away spider webs—equally unpleasant but easier to see through. Familiarity can be a friend.

Once again, after long weeks of injecting hormones, my eggs were removed, fertilized, and two healthy embryos were implanted inside me.

"They look strong," Dr. Holzer said. "This is a good sign."

"I hope you're right."

"We shall hope together then," he said.

Dr. Holzer's face was so open and sympathetic you almost had to believe him. I lay there, willing those embryos to live, staring up at the ceiling of the procedure room, machines beeping, nurses in white masks looking down at me with caring eyes, Enrico's hand in mine.

At that time, it took two weeks after the fertilized embryos were returned into the womb that you returned for a pregnancy test. Two weeks after that you returned for the result. A month of hoping, praying, believing, begging, bargaining.

A month later, we dragged those long, disagreeable days behind us and sat waiting in the doctor's office again. I was nervous and tense and pressed my palms against my belly hoping that if a baby grew inside me he would feel the full weight of my wanting. Dr. Holzer arrived, dropped heavily into the chair before us and, for a moment, said nothing. The hope offered months ago faded right there and then in the gulf between us, disintegrating like old, fragile paper. Our pregnancy test had come back. It was negative again. There would be no baby.

We were living loss upon loss, piling them up like trash in a junkyard, scraps of metal, old cars, filth, and waste in a barren land. Enrico and I wandered around that place, navigating the clutter, searching for a way out. I bowed my head, clutching defeat close, drowning in what felt like another monumental failure.

"We can stop," Enrico said, holding me close. "We don't need children to be happy. If you don't want to do this anymore, we won't."

"It just feels like if we stop, where do we go from here?"

I knew that if he could, Enrico would have gladly shouldered the burden, heavy as it was. Whatever hope existed was dim, a fire burning just enough to keep the embers red. But it was there, so I clung to its warmth. I returned to my eternally optimistic doctor and agreed to try another round of IVF. Then I walked back toward that uninviting scrap yard, looking for something I had lost along the way.

7 Flashes of Light in a Dark Sky

Our third round of IVF worked. I was pregnant.

There was life inside me again. Family and friends were thrilled, grateful to see some distance between us and sorrow. It allowed more room for them. The pregnancy opened a gargantuan space inside that made me feel buoyant. We had earned every moment of that feeling, had fought for it, and were entitled to it, so I clung tightly. It wasn't that past hurts were erased, I knew I would carry those always. It's more that they changed shape, softened, and felt less jagged and sharp.

That positive pregnancy test might have been a good opportunity to cultivate those lessons of letting go. To enjoy our happiness minus the firm grip. It was an opportune moment to remember that nothing is permanent and that life can never be controlled. But those yogic lessons were pushed to the edge of my vision, still visible but not quite in focus, because I was choosing not to see. All I saw was the future I wanted so desperately.

No matter how hard I fought to carry and care for a child, the fight alone was never going to be enough. It's what I couldn't control that was deciding my fate.

Back in the clinic for a routine follow-up appointment, the technician put the ultrasound to my belly and said something I will never forget. "There is no heartbeat."

My world stopped. Even dust particles seemed to hover in mid air. I couldn't blink or feel or think. And then in one swift intake of breath, the world started up again, the dust fell to the floor, and the weight of that inconceivable sentence squeezed the life out of me again. I literally could not stop myself from falling, face in my hands, bawling my eyes out for the baby I wanted so badly but could not seem to have.

Several nurses crowded around me, but I wouldn't or couldn't speak to anyone. Dr. Holzer arrived and demanded, "What is going on here?"

He guided me, a hand holding my elbow, down a long, narrow hallway into his office. Enrico walked beside me but I could not look at him. I knew the anguish that would be in his eyes and I felt responsible for its presence. We sat in uncomfortable chairs, disbelief forming pools of muddy water at our feet.

"Tarah, some embryos take longer to develop," Dr. Holzer explained. "It's still very possible that this is a viable pregnancy."

I said nothing.

"It's too soon to give up, do you hear me?"

He told us to hold on, and scheduled another test in seven days, his clear blue eyes betraying nothing. "Get some rest."

But rest did not come. At night I lay by my husband and begged God to help our baby live, whispering quietly to that dormant embryo, pleading with it to come to life.

And very unexpectedly, it did.

When we went back for that second test, it was not death we faced, but life. Dr. Holzer found not one heartbeat, but two. The heart of that embryo had not only started beating, it had split in half, creating two lives out of one. I was elated. My doctor, though, looked displeased. It wasn't good news.

"It's very unusual for an embryo to split this late," he said. "It would be a very dangerous pregnancy."

Dangerous, because the babies, who would be identical, would develop in the same amniotic sac. As they grew in such a limited space, one child risked getting strangled by the umbilical cord.

"If they live to four months, *if*," Dr. Holzer cautioned, "you would have to be on full bed rest and constant monitoring for the duration of your pregnancy."

He believed it was too risky and encouraged me to terminate.

"We can try again," he said.

I listened politely, but I would have cut off my own arm before letting go of these babies. I would do whatever I had to do.

I was pregnant for just over fourteen weeks.

Those heartbeats, tiny flashes of white on an ultrasound machine, a sing-song melody made by two twinkling stars in a black night, simply went out. Their hearts stopped. Having lived as long they were able, they made one final beat and then no other. I demanded to see the ultrasound, needing to see for myself that those bright flashes had gone dark. I saw only grey shadows inside of my womb. It was as empty and desolate as a far-off planet no humans would ever want to visit.

"It happens," Dr. Holzer said sadly, touching my arm. "They just weren't strong enough."

I was devastated. My body miscarried, flushing away our dreams. Enrico and I continued our long walk through a tunnel that seemed to have no end—or, if there was one, it was impossible to see.

"What do you want to do now?" Enrico asked. "Tell me what you want, and we'll do it." He was looking to me, needing some kind of answer that offered possibility.

We had been saving financially for everything that a baby would bring. We saved for the IVF treatments, which had yet to receive government funding, we saved for a car we thought we needed, we saved for that coveted nest egg. But at that moment, I didn't care about any of it.

"I want to go to Italy," I told him.

So we did.

8 Under the Bridges of Venice

There would be no talk of children in Italy. For three weeks we let go of the load we had been carrying since not long after our wedding. Guilt and shame are heavy. So is sorrow. Every obstacle became a link that connected us, making what we had unbreakable.

Perhaps it was the strange streets, the lack of responsibility, the food, the wine, the sleeping in, the smell of fresh coffee—slowly I began to feel lighter, less weighed down by my circumstance. Getting away from our home, away from an empty room that was meant to have a crib and lemon-coloured walls, was the only path that offered any peace. It may have been as simple as a much-needed vacation, but ultimately it was a desperate escape from our life and from the all-consuming desire to have a child. Being unable to carry to term tainted everything—every dinner out, every walk in the park, every gathering with friends. The wanting was always there.

In Italy there was freedom and distraction. I even let a charming Italian man in Rome named Stefano, who wore a burgundy scarf over a teal blazer, cut my hair. It had grown long and I was ready to let it go. It was a spontaneous decision while walking down the street one day. I saw Stefano through a salon window laughing at something, and walked in, drawn to the sound.

"Cut it off, please."

"Short?" he asked, full of excitement.

"Not too short," I clarified.

"Sit, sweet lady," he laughed.

He led me to a chair like he was escorting me to a dance floor, then touched my cheek affectionately before picking up his scissors. I closed my eyes, eager to see someone new in the mirror. Walking back toward our rented apartment, I met Enrico in the cobbled streets.

"You seem younger. Do you like it?" he asked.

"I do."

"It's been a long time since I've felt anywhere near this happy. Is it because we're far from home?" Enrico asked.

"We're far from everything. That was the point."

We travelled from city to city, holding hands, renting small apartments with windows that looked out onto landscapes that were nothing like our own views. It helped to see things differently. And that helped to bring back a softness between us.

"Come with me," Enrico said.

"Where are we going?" I asked.

"To do something everyone has to do in Venice," he said, pulling me toward a bridge.

"Not a gondola ride? That's so touristy!"

"I don't care," he said. "We're here, we may never come back, and I want to sit in a gondola with you. We're doing this."

Romantic gestures are like wildflowers, beautiful and tender to the touch.

"How do we choose the driver?" I wondered.

"Go with your gut," he said. "Or, knowing you, you'll interview them and decide based on their answers."

He was right, of course. I spoke to many until Marco captured my attention. He was wearing a blue and white striped shirt and a black beret. We negotiated a price, then

Enrico guided me into the gondola. At least for a while, we could sail away.

"This is incredible," he said.

Marco sang Italian love songs as he rowed under bridges we could almost reach up and touch.

"I wish I could record this," Enrico whispered. "So I can watch it again whenever I want to remember."

I put my head on his shoulder and looked at the sky.

"You are my happiness," I said to him. I knew it was true, that not one moment of the last few years would have been survivable without him.

Many of the churches in Italy are large and ornate, but we sought out places of worship that had nondescript facades. In one, in the Trastevere district of Rome, we burned candles for the lives we had lost. One for our first son and two for the twins. It was the only moment during which we allowed ourselves to revisit our wounds. It was letting the memories push up through layers of muscle until they throbbed like a headache. In a wooden pew surrounded by stained glass, each time I shifted in my seat it was like leaning on a bad bruise. I put my head in my hands and prayed for the ability to find my way to the other side, even though I had no idea where that was.

"Let's go now," I insisted. "We need to go."

Enrico got up without a word and followed me out of the church that smelled of candle wax and furniture polish. We pushed open the doors and let the candles we lit burn away.

"Let's go grab dinner and a good bottle of wine," he said.

The path to healing comes with time. You need to walk forward and stay focused for as long as it takes to get there. Italy became the diversion we badly needed. We dined at trattorias in hidden alleys in Rome, admired the Uffizi in Florence, explored the unearthed remains of Pompeii, stood in awe atop the still-smoking Mount Vesuvius, stared at the sea in Positano, and savoured the best pizza in Naples.

We left Italy reluctantly. Something new had been cultivated there, some seed of possibility that we had found and wanted to smuggle back. Boarding our plane, we saw hockey star Sidney Crosby chatting with the ticket agent. I felt relieved, a plane carrying Sidney Crosby could not possibly crash.

9 Come Find Me in the Cosmos

I met Peter in the most unexpected way.

He came to be an invaluable mentor in managing sadness, a term he came by through his own heartache. While it took years for our friendship to take the shape that it did, the seed was planted on a reporting shift one May that began like any other.

As a journalist, you rarely know what kind of day you are going to have, what kind of assignment you're going to get, or whom you will meet. The not knowing is exciting. The days can be hectic and unforgiving, and most reporters know what it feels like to get their news piece done with about 90 seconds to spare before it goes to air. Dealing with that kind of pressure is not for everyone. It's a job unlike any other and I thrived in it.

My assignment on that day in May was to follow up on the death of a young volunteer firefighter. He had been killed almost one year ago while on duty during a training exercise in the Quebec town where he lived. He was only twenty years old. The Quebec's Workers Safety Board had just released its findings, which essentially determined what went wrong and how to prevent it from happening again. I needed to explain the findings, interview someone from the Safety Board, talk to the young man's fire chief, and more importantly, his family.

It's never easy to ask parents who have lost a child to speak to the media. We approach homes encased with mourning and ask for just a few words. Occasionally they oblige, often they don't. They don't usually even open the door.

Peter is that young firefighter's father. Still aching from his son's death, he agreed to speak with every reporter who had asked for an interview that day. He understood that daily news is time sensitive, and if he wanted to have a voice, it had to be when the coroner's findings were released. Tomorrow, a new headline would capture the attention of a constantly moving news cycle.

When Peter stepped up to the microphones to speak, there it was again: lived-in grief. Once you've seen it up close, it's unmistakable.

I saw the same hollow look of loss that I had seen in Katie's mother. That hurt-filled stare, as if he was gazing up from the bottom of a musty well. I sought Peter out before we left that day, wanting to let him know how sorry I was for his loss. I had not yet encountered my own. At that time, I was simply a witness. Peter accepted my condolences quietly. Strangely, I asked if I could hug him goodbye. He said yes, and then I left.

I never expected to cross paths with him again, but he would come back into my life almost three years later with an email at work. I wasn't sure who it was from at first: I didn't recognize the name, and the subject line read simply, "Thank you, long overdue."

He wrote that the quiet words we had exchanged after our interview that day had stayed with him. That the compassion he felt was something he still remembered, and he simply wanted me to know that he was grateful. He wanted nothing in return.

That email arrived when Enrico and I had begun trying to get pregnant again, and it wasn't working. The relief of Italy had faded with another embryo that had lived but a few short months. Peter's words were a kind of balm. I knew almost nothing about this man, but I could see he understood sorrow better than anyone in my life except my husband. It was as if Peter dove below the surface of my sadness and pulled me up for air when I couldn't breathe.

"You said that we who have lost children are different, changed somehow," Peter wrote. Those had been my words all those years ago. I still have no idea why I said that to him.

"Thanks for looking and seeing," his note continued. "That innocuous but deeply human comment about change was more important than you probably could have imagined. It helped me realize a couple of things, mostly that there are so many others who lose children and we're not as alone as we may feel. Secondly, that we had indeed changed and must learn to accept and live with that change."

Who was this man, I asked myself? A father who had lived through the unimaginable, and now, for some reason, was speaking directly to me.

"What are you going to do?" Enrico asked.

"I don't know, but I feel like I can trust him. It seems like too much of a coincidence, him reaching out now."

"I can understand that," he said. "What will you say to him?"

"The truth, I guess. Somehow, I think he might be able to help."

"Help how?" Enrico asked.

"Help us find a way to live with what life has dealt us. Help us to move on?"

After printing out Peter's letter and keeping it close to me for several days, I finally wrote back. I thanked him, and in return shared a private glimpse of what Enrico and I had been living. In many ways, it was easier because Peter was a stranger. I was able to say things to him that I couldn't say to those I loved.

"I don't recognize myself when I look in the mirror," I wrote to him.

"Grief has changed you," Peter answered. "It has altered you, in your core. But you are still there."

Our first email exchange led to dozens more. We communicated through words, and I came to place my aching heart in his hands, believing that it was a safe place to put it. Safe enough to reveal, despite my job and my status as a television personality, that I felt broken.

Peter said I needed to believe that I would once again embrace life. That distance and time would ease the pressure of loss. He knew this because he had lived it.

"Tarah, one of the greatest challenges is looking sadness in the eye until you know it can't hurt you anymore."

Peter was able to do that, whereas I was turning away from grief, because staring at it made my eyes water. Peter offered understanding, but he also offered hope. If he had survived, so could we.

"Survival to me is about becoming stronger," he wrote. "Few of us get through life without challenges."

Peter was my own personal Dalai Lama. He once referred to himself as a "casual tow-truck driver for a few random souls I found crashed near my path." I remain eternally grateful that he spotted my collision.

Peter and I never met in person again, but our friendship lives on. It's always with words.

"If you ever need me, just tug the cosmos that connected us. If that doesn't work, email me."

10 Embers

If you have ever seen firefighters in motion, there is a grace to their movements. Get too close or take one step too many, and you will disrupt a flawlessly organized ritual they have practised. There is something soothing about watching them work, even within the frenzied process of putting out fire.

"The father and his young son made it to the door," explained the fire chief to reporters. "They didn't have the strength to open it. In that sense, they never had a chance."

I was assigned to cover an overnight fire. It had erupted from a pot of oil on the stove. The flames quickly climbed drapes, consumed wooden cabinets, and moved to the roof where it sought out the oxygen needed to keep burning. Once the largest flames had been put out, the firefighters in soot-covered gear worked on dousing hot spots from hoses fat with water.

From a safe distance behind yellow tape, neighbours sat on front stoops or stared out from balconies. With coats and blankets pulled around their shoulders, they shook their heads in disbelief and shock. Others came from down the block, drawn by the sound of sirens. Parents held their children, and children clenched their dolls. Strangers lined the streets standing shoulder to shoulder, watching.

As a journalist, covering a fire is often about covering the aftermath. On a quiet Montreal street just after dawn, my job, along with a camera person, was to find the people who could help tell the story of what had happened. Perhaps a mother who had woken to the sound of screaming and ran for her own children, or a neighbour who had been among the first to see thick smoke pouring from the window, or a stranger who had been offering consolatory coats and condolences. With words and video, we pieced together a moment in time when the lives of the living had forever changed.

"The mother survived the fire," said the fire chief.

"Is she badly injured?" I asked.

"She's alive," he said. "That's all I know."

When asked how old the child was, he answered with the air of a man who had seen far too much tragedy in his life. "He was six."

An overcome neighbour hunched on his front steps. "She brought me casseroles for my dinner," he whispered of the mother. "How could this happen?"

"It's not fair," he continued. "They were such nice people."

I crouched next to a father sitting on a curb, his son held tightly in his arms. "It could have happened to any of us," he said. "That could just as easily have been my home, my son."

"Why did you come?" I asked. "You didn't know them."

"To see," he said. "To be here. Aren't we all a family in times like this?"

An older woman wearing a lavender housecoat and a flowered head cover shook her head and glanced toward the sky. "I used to watch them coming and going," she said, arms folded in front of her.

"How will she go on?" she turned and asked me. So many questions with no good answers.

Where is that mother now, I wonder, and has she found a way to live in a world without her family? Where would they be if that first spark had never ignited? If fire hadn't burned away one possible future, leaving a tragic path in its place?

11 The Way Forward

I was kicking off my shoes as I checked the message on my phone. When I heard who it was, I froze. I pressed the play button again. I listened to the message a third time. Then I saved it.

Climbing the stairs two by two I found Enrico in his office. He is a translator and works with words. He loves them.

"Did you get the message?" I asked.

"I did," he said. "We have a lot to talk about."

When we first began IVF treatments, I had also placed our names on a number of adoption waiting lists. I didn't know if it would come to that, but it seemed like the smart thing to do. We had been told adoption could take years. Shockingly, by the time the call did come, three long years had passed. A Quebec adoption agency working with South Korea explained that our names were now at the top of the list, and they weren't giving us much time to decide if we'd like to proceed. There are hundreds of families eager to take your place if you decline, they said. While we didn't know what the process consisted of, we knew that at the end of it, we could be parents.

"Let's go for a walk," said my husband.

We walked through the trees with thick branches and shapely green leaves that draped over grassy fields in Lafontaine Park. Fat grey squirrels stopped us in our tracks with their beady eyes, demanding food.

"What do you think?" I asked him, impatient to begin the discussion.

"It's a big decision," he answered. "It's strange to have to decide so quickly about something so important."

"We have one round of in vitro left," I said. "What if we just didn't do it? What if we did this instead?"

"Do you remember one of the first walks we took through this park?" he asked. "When we first began dating."

"When we talked about having children?"

"You were the one who talked about children," he went on. "You told me you wanted to have two children: one biological and one adopted."

"I guess that didn't exactly work out as planned."

"Part of it could still work out."

"Yes, it could."

We continued to talk for several hours. Choosing international adoption meant closing one door and opening another. It meant letting go of having a child biologically and all that goes along with it. We would never see our features reflected in our baby, and we would never know exactly from whom our child came. I would never be pregnant and give birth. Adoption meant letting go of what we thought life *would* be and opening up to what *could* be.

"The idea of not going through our last IVF treatment is pretty appealing," I admitted. "I don't really want to do it again."

"I know," he said. "I understand."

I pressed on. "And there would be a baby out there for us. We could have our baby."

We turned the corner onto Sherbrooke, a picturesque street lined with old, stone buildings and dotted with art galleries and high-end clothing stores. The city was alive and breathing. We slowed down and watched it and contemplated how each road we walk down, each choice that we make leads to a thousand possible other ones. As we walked, I watched people in cars, on the bus, on the streets, kissing their children, and walking their dogs, and marvelled at how each of us, billions of humans, live our lives hoping to find as much happiness as we can. I wondered if we also sometimes hold ourselves back from that happiness out of uncertainty, or anger, or fear.

Something changed inside me, something settled, the way sediment drifts and eventually touches down on the ocean floor. Within all that movement, I felt surprisingly still. And, it seems, so did Enrico.

"I think we should do it," he said. "I think this is the way we become parents."

"I think so too. It's like a knowing." Never had such simple sentences meant so much or been so true.

The way forward had been chosen.

My mother always says the toughest part of any choice is making it. That part was done. Never, though, did I imagine the road beyond that choice would be as bumpy as it turned out to be.

12 Abiding Time

For all the children in the world needing a family, I somehow imagined that the process of adoption would be easier. And certainly faster. But considering how long it took for that first phone call to happen, I should have known that we were in store for life lessons in patience and perseverance.

At the adoption agency, our file was opened, and we signed a contract. And so began an entire year filled with the signing and filling out of countless forms. There were medical tests to take and financial considerations, as the cost of international adoption is significant. We collected reference letters from friends and colleagues. We attended mandatory classes about the adoption process and what to expect once we left for South Korea and took custody of our child.

Most onerous were the hours of evaluation by a social worker who assessed us as suitable parents—or not. We met her together on a number of occasions, then individually, and then she came to our home. She asked us about our childhoods, how we met, what our relationship was like, what our previous relationships were like, why we wanted to become parents, and what kind of child, healthy or ill, we were willing to accept. The process was endless and infuriating. I understood the need to ensure that children are adopted into safe and healthy homes, but this was excessive. I wanted to scream, *Enough already! Just sign the goddamn forms. Can't you see we're good people? No one makes you go down such a gruelling path when you can have a baby naturally.* Instead, we sat politely and answered all of her questions, digging as far back into our pasts as she chose to excavate.

Throughout the months it took to complete our file, there was never any talk of a child, only a distant, intangible promise of one. Once the papers were assembled and sent off, what lay ahead was more waiting. And waiting is hard. The days seemed longer. Every phone call was potentially *the* call. Impatience burrowed into my skin and crawled around, making me jumpy. People constantly told us to just live our lives while the process ran its course. I tried. We tried. But the truth is that I still always felt like I was waiting.

More than a year passed. And then six more months after that. Still, there was no news. It's difficult not to get discouraged, impossible not to revisit old wounds. We put off travelling, just in case. The days came and went without any momentum to move us forward.

That kind of waiting takes its toll. It chips away at resilience; it erases the clean edges of optimism and makes them blurry. A distance settles in, a gulf between the life you have and the life you want. Shiny toys, a baby stroller, a chocolate brown diaper bag: all gifts from friends and family who threw us baby showers. The packages sat unopened and unused, gathering dust. It was as if the further away we got from those first moments of excitement, the less real a baby began to feel.

"I'm worried that when we finally get that phone call," Enrico said, "we will have changed too much."

I didn't say anything.

"I'm afraid that we're putting our lives on hold," he said. "That in some ways we've stopped living. I'm worried that once that call comes, I'll feel differently."

The hope we had fought for was abandoning him. It had slipped away some place unsavoury after too many months of lying still. Somewhere along the way, living in a limbo that pushes you into all kinds of nasty places, my husband had begun giving up and had started to move on. I didn't know how to give him back what life was taking away.

"Don't give up," I begged him. "Not yet."

I called the adoption agency and pleaded for information. They were always kind, no doubt I was far from the only one who felt desperate and adrift. During one conversation, a woman working on our file said something I've never forgotten.

She said, "I know it feels long Tarah, but when you hold your baby in your arms, it will all make sense."

I felt a tightness inside my chest, as if the intensity of wanting would catapult my soul from my body like a slingshot, breaking me wide open.

"Why will it make sense?"

"Because you will know, beyond any doubt, that the baby you get was meant to be yours. You will know it profoundly. And if it takes one or two more years, it won't have mattered, because you'll know it was all for him."

After hanging up, I let every last tear fall, emptying me of longing. I would hold on to her words, because I needed them. I would believe, for myself and for my husband, that our baby was out there, and that what we needed to do was to wait for him.

So, we waited.

13 What One Day Brings

"I have some pictures of your son."

Finally. Just under two years after signing our adoption contract, there was a baby.

It is a strange feeling to want something for so long that when it finally happens, it takes a moment for the waiting to drain out of your bones. It's like being in a dark room for too long. When the light is turned on your eyes need time to adjust.

It was early morning and the adoption agency promised to send us the electronic file right away. It contained photos, a medical history, an evaluation of his progress and all the information they had on his birth parents. I was elated. My husband, though, was struggling with uncertainty. Time had bred doubt and it had propagated.

Enrico had so often been the anchor that I clung to, but now he was the one who needed my help to keep him from floating away. He needed me to remind him that if we didn't both want to go forward with the adoption, then we would both stay exactly where we were.

"I love you," I said, "and if you don't want to do this, then we won't."

"I don't want to deprive you of becoming a mother, especially after so long, after everything we've been through."

"You are what's most important to me," I said. "I can't and won't do this without you." It was the truth.

I couldn't judge his uncertainty.

"Open the file and read about him," I said as I left for work. "I'll talk to you tonight."

The adoption agency had given us until the end of the day to decide. It would have to be enough.

"I can't be the one making this decision," he said.

"Trust yourself. You'll know what to do."

My commitment had never wavered, and now he had to find his way back to his own. I wanted to beg, plead, cajole him back to a place of knowing. I prayed that he would.

I honestly can't remember other details of that day. I know I went to work and reported on a story, but I have no idea what it was about. When I told family and a few friends that I hadn't yet opened the file, no one could believe it. I couldn't put myself through that if at the end of the day Enrico was to decide that he couldn't move forward with this.

He and I usually spoke during the day, but I didn't phone or contact him. Time crawled. It took an incredible amount of mental energy to keep my thoughts from lingering on the child—what he looked like, who he was, when he was born.

The day finally ended and I called Enrico to tell him I was heading home. "I'll meet you outside your work in fifteen minutes," he said.

I kissed him hello and searched for a sign, a clue to help me decipher what he would not say out loud. Did he seem happier or more stressed? He was like a skilled magician keeping his secrets safe, giving nothing away. He didn't mention the adoption, the baby, the file, or the future. Unsure of what kind of conversation was imminent, I felt ill.

When we arrived home, he led me up to his office. He pulled me onto his lap, stared into my eyes and still said nothing. Then he broke from our gaze to open a file on his computer. At the same time, music began. It was "Lost Together" by Blue Rodeo.

And then there he was. A little boy with a head full of hair and chocolate-coloured eyes. He was wearing a blue and white striped T-shirt and sitting in a bright pink chair. "This is our son," he said. "This is our child."

Curled in my husband's arms, I bawled my eyes out for a long, long time.

14 He Comes from My Heart

I carried a picture of our son around with me, a constant reminder that he was real and he was ours. He lived a world away, but he was still our baby. Knowing that helped me to breathe.

We framed pictures and hung them on our walls, we cleaned off toys, and chose colours for his room that reminded me of the inside of a lime. We pieced back together what had been broken, because we now had someone to build it for again. Old scars didn't disappear, but they faded. Enrico and I had changed, but we were learning to accept the changes. Maybe one day we would even come to love them. I was going to be a mother. Knowing that was enough.

My nieces were four and six years old and had many questions for me, the innocent, sweet, concerns of the young.

"Where was the baby that was inside your belly?" Sarah asked.

"Oh, he's an angel now."

"An angel?" she exclaimed. "We want to be angels too!"

"You are angels," I explained. "Angels on earth. First, though, you have to live as precious girls."

"Why didn't he get to live?" they pressed.

"Because our baby needed to care for other angels," I told them. "So, he left before we wanted him to."

Apprehensively, she asked, "Will you ever see him again?"

"I want to," I answered.

Explaining that we were adopting a baby, one who had been born halfway around the world, inspired yet more delicate questions.

"But how can he be your baby if he didn't come out of your belly?" Sarah asked. "And will he be our real cousin?"

I pulled both of my nieces into my arms. The younger one, Kalilah, was bobbing her head vigorously as if those questions had been baffling her as well. Her large eyes were made bigger by her thick, purple glasses.

"Well, he didn't come out of my belly, but he'll come from my heart."

"Is that possible?" they asked me, their eyes widening.

"Absolutely," I answered.

We waited for him together, as a family.

I wish I could tell you that we got on a plane and left soon after all the legalities were dealt with. But the wheels of adoption move at a sloth-like pace. Governments are involved, as are court systems, and social welfare agencies. What were we waiting for this time? One final phone call, the one telling us it was time to leave for Seoul. It was late May, our adoption agency told us we should expect to leave no later than October.

So again, we waited.

15 Let There Be No More Talk of Loss

Montreal's deliciously hot summer had come and gone. Autumn arrived. Just as the leaves had changed colour, turning trees into fields of blazing sunsets, the long-promised phone call arrived.

Enrico was home. I know he would rather have been anywhere else. I also know that having to call and tell me what was said was one of the toughest moments of his life. I was at work, covering a story in a town about an hour outside of Montreal. When I answered his call, Enrico's voice cracked like an old record recorded long ago. I heard him take a breath. I closed my eyes.

"We're not getting the baby," he said. "The birth mother… has changed her mind."

When you've looked loss in the eyes once, you know what to expect when you see it again. It's like muscle memory. I was about to be thrown back into an unmistakable hell. A metal door, inches thick, slammed shut. I felt it close around me, thick and impenetrable as a bank vault that shoots up and locks into place when a panic switch is pulled. I could almost see the large wheel lock turning and securing in place.

No, no, no, no, no. Please, no.

The pressure of what those words meant pounded against me, demanding to be acknowledged. I was breaking. There was nothing I could do to stop it. It felt as if my ribs cracked, snapping in two as easily as dried branches. I heard the cameraman asking me what was wrong, but my entire body was clenched like a muscle in spasm. And then the dam broke, ripping away my metal wall as if tossing aside a piece of tin. I started to weep.

Our baby isn't coming. Our son belongs to someone else. I'm not going to be a mother. Not this time.

Enrico was at the top of the steps, waiting for me at home. His skin was pale, his eyes were red-rimmed, his lashes were wet and stuck together. It was a face drained of every drop of joy. Grief had reared its ugly head once more.

"How?" he asked.

How? Why? This can't fucking be happening.

We closed the doors and windows and caged ourselves in once again. Our liquifying insides keeping us immobile. Through that sludge, we swallowed the disbelief that comes from knowing the life you were so close to having has been ripped from you, again. We took down frames and hid them in drawers we would not open, perhaps ever. Then I curled up on the couch, not sure when I would move again.

My sister and mother showed up a few hours later and wrapped me in their arms. As we sat at the kitchen table, I felt like a zombie. I could see their faces, but from a distance. I felt deserted and uninhabitable and very, very lonely.

The adoption agency workers in Montreal and Seoul felt terrible about what had happened. It was only the second time in their decades-long relationship that a birth mother had returned in the final stages of an adoption. The baby's biological mother was only nineteen years old, and I knew she must have been tormented over letting him go. In all my devastation, I felt only compassion for her. If she had changed her mind, even a week later, he would have been gone, and perhaps she would have spent her entire life mourning her child. Some part of me was glad that she was able to have him. He was hers, after all, before he was ours.

Every molecule of my body felt imprinted with sadness. I had no choice but to bear it, but how do you bear it? How do you live through grief when the hope you carried within you is tethered to something flying away? Do you let it go?

Enrico and I had been here before. We had found a love that grows from woeful places, we had mourned together and discovered that immense compassion can come from those places. And it is beautiful. In many ways, loss shows you who you truly are. We knew the road that lay before us, and we knew what it would take to walk it. There would be solace somewhere, eventually, but not for a while. I had to go on faith that it would be there, if I simply began putting one foot in front of the other.

Hope

16 Even the Fiercest Fall

The funeral home was a stand-alone building made of large, rectangular stones, windows with wide frames, and a roof that reached up into a precise point. There were patches of grass on either side of a half-dozen concrete steps that led up to double doors whose giant handles were made of inky-coloured metal. The door handles had been touched and pulled over long years by hundreds of palms moist with sorrow. A shiny gold cross, affixed to the roof, gleamed in the early winter sun that felt warm as noon approached. Inside, thin curtains with decorative holes along the edges swayed in a delicate breeze at the slightly open windows. A family standing at attention stood off to the side in mourning before the corpse of a twenty-three year old man.

Our newsroom had decided to produce a piece on the controversy brewing over energy drinks. More and more of them were hitting the market, their list of ingredients and the high caffeine content of concern to some. There was no proof that these drinks had caused harm in any way, but a number of parents in both Canada and the United States had spoken out after their children had died suddenly. Teens and young people were the target demographic and the primary consumers.

While researching our story, we came across an article in a Quebec newspaper about a father who was convinced that energy drinks had contributed to the death of his son. I had tried to contact him by phone but only succeeded in reaching his wife. She told me about the funeral arrangements and assured me he would call back. He didn't. We decided to go anyway.

That's how we ended up in a remote Quebec town at a funeral for a young man we didn't know. We were there because of that twenty-three year old man's father, Jean Gabriel. But not only had I not been invited, it was likely that my presence would be unwelcome and unappreciated. I was steeling myself, fully prepared for the possibility of being thrown out.

"Here we go," I said to the cameraman, Christophe, who stood at my side.

The handle was warm when I pulled at it. Inside, it was dimly lit and smelled of fresh flowers and something damp. We looked around quickly. No one came to greet us so we found an empty room, went inside and closed the door.

"You stay here," I said to Christophe. "But be ready. If he speaks to us, it will be quick. You need to be set up."

"Do you think he'll talk to you?" he asked.

"I have absolutely no idea," I said.

"Good luck."

"I definitely need it."

The viewing room where the vigil was taking place was surrounded by panels of shiny chestnut-coloured wood. Bouquets of flowers, tall and small, were huddled in one corner like guests. Delicate, white cards scribbled with sympathetic words clung to the stems like petals. The lights were dimmed. A coffin lay near the back wall. Inside was the body of Maxime Gabriel dressed in jeans and a white dress shirt striped with thin blue lines, his eyes closed, his skin the colour of pale peaches. He looked like he was sleeping.

In front of the coffin in the centre of the room, people sat in cushioned chairs, looking tired and confused. Jean Gabriel was easy to spot. He was a more compact man than his son, thin and taut, but his presence was large and took up a lot of space. He was clearly the patriarch of the family. I watched him for a few moments, sensing that he had not had an easy life. His hair was thinning and pulled back in a low ponytail. His face was covered in wrinkles, each crease wide and full of stories. His eyes were a piercing, pale blue.

"Excuse me," I said in French as I approached. "I'm so sorry to intrude, but may I have a moment?"

"Who are you?" asked Mr. Gabriel. I clearly did not belong.

I explained who I was and why I was there. As I spoke, family members took up positions on either side of him as if preparing for a fight. The attacks from his grown children came quickly.

"You should not be here," they hissed.

"You are not welcome," said one. "Get out!"

"You were not invited!" said another. *"Va t'en!"* Go away.

He said nothing for several minutes, then raised his hand.

They were dry and rope-like veins bulged from his skin.

"Silence!" he said. With his palm still in the air, everyone who had been speaking went instantly quiet.

The fragile skin under his eyes was heavy from lack of sleep. Mr. Gabriel was grieving, his anguish so fresh it had not yet found a place to settle. I felt that I could touch it, so familiar was I with that feeling. I did not look away from him, and I did not say another word.

"Je vais vous parler," he said. I will talk to you.

I am not sure what this man saw during those moments of quiet, or why he made the decision he did. But contrary to his family's wishes, Jean Gabriel agreed to answer my questions.

"You will have five minutes," he said. "And then you will leave."

We walked back toward the room where Christophe stood expectantly. There were two chairs facing each other. I sat in one and Mr. Gabriel sank wearily into the other. Christophe nodded imperceptibly, which told me he had begun recording.

"He drank too many of those drinks," he said, "and the caffeine, it affected him, it made him sick." Mr. Gabriel had nothing but his own conviction. His answers were concise and to the point.

"What will you do now?" I asked him. "Will you continue to speak out?"

"No," he said. "I have nothing more to say."

Death takes something from even the fiercest among us. I am not sure what kind of father he was, perhaps firm and unapologetic, but it was clear that his family was where his armour was at its weakest.

"That's my boy in there," he said. "My boy. And because he's dead, a part of me is dead now too."

From those pale eyes, giant tears welled up. They leaked into the folds of his face, sliding down until, eventually, with no place left to cling too, dripped reluctantly away.

This was a man who did not show vulnerability often. He dropped his head, inhaled a slow, wet breath, and I knew our interview was over. The moist marks still visible on his face were faint reminders of what death can leave behind. Hesitating, I touched his hand. He took mine in his and squeezed gently but his gaze never left the floor. He pulled himself from the chair, wiped his eyes and, in a voice I could not have disobeyed, ordered me to stay away from the church service that would follow.

"No cameras there," he said to me. "You can film, as long as I can't see you. *Est-ce que tu me comprends*?" Do you understand me?

"I do," I said. "Thank you. I am truly sorry. For your loss."

Jean Gabriel looked at me for a brief moment then turned and walked back to be by his son. His gait was laborious, as if his hips stung with each step.

"Are you OK?" Christophe asked. It had been only a few days since the adoption was cancelled, and he had been in the van with me when Enrico's phone call came.

"I'm fine. Let's go," I said to him. "We need to get set up, but you heard what he said—whatever you do, don't let him see you."

Two blocks from the funeral home, parked on a side street lined with trees, Christophe used a strong zoom lens to capture the Gabriel family making the long slow climb up the steps into their church for the funeral service. They disappeared behind big, wooden doors, their coats were pulled up and around their bodies against a chill that had blown into the air.

17 Acceptance Will Find You

Enrico and I were as unmoving as stone. It was as if a fine dust had settled over us. When we did move, I was sure that if the light caught us just right you could see a white powder lift then slowly drift back down. That's how still we were.

The cumulative loss of so many babies had left an ache inside of me. I stared out at a world with no colour, only varying shades of dingy. With every defeat it felt as if parts of me were breaking off and dropping away. I left them there and knew that I would never find them again. The farther away I walked, the less I remembered what those pieces felt like when they were a part of me.

Like I had done so many times before, I sought out the comfort of my thank-god-I-have-you yoga teacher Antoine. Sitting quietly on my mat while others left at the end of the class, Antoine would see me, walk over and sit cross legged in the place beside me. He often let many minutes of silence pass before saying a word.

"Let yourself feel, Tarah," said Antoine. "The only way to pass through sadness is to allow it to be. No one is expecting you to be happy. So let go of the struggle of *trying* to be happy, and accept your sadness. It's there. You might as well go and meet it."

"I'm tired of feeling sad," I said. "I want to feel something else."

"Are you really feeling it? Or are you running from it? Be still. Sit with your sadness and give it the space that it needs. Welcome it as part of you. It will pass. All things do. That's the good news," he said, grinning.

Feel it. Welcome it.

I tried. Most days it didn't work, but I tried. I set aside time every day to be still with the feelings I had worked so hard at avoiding: disappointment, despair. It was brutal. But eventually, that quiet space where I came face-to-face with my sadness opened a new way of seeing. An acceptance of all the parts of myself, including the parts that were struggling. By allowing the tough feelings a place to *be*, I felt more in control and less chaotic. And when I found—and continue to find—those moments of stillness, even if I am mourning, it is the most at ease I ever feel.

Staring at myself in the mirror was still unpleasant. I was sure I appeared different, was different. I was afraid those I loved could see that.

I wondered if Peter had ever felt that way. How did he see himself after the death of his son? Our email correspondence grew quickly from those first tentative notes. He became among my most trusted confidants. It happened often that when I needed someone the most, an email would turn up within hours, asking if I was OK.

"I didn't want to see the damage so I didn't look," Peter wrote.

"Do you ever worry that the person you have become is *less* somehow?" I asked him. Writing to him was like sending messages to an unseen spirit guide who knew exactly what I needed to hear.

"Time, Tarah, will bring a new vision of yourself," Peter wrote. "Life always prevails. Who we were before has been rendered irrelevant by both the journey life chooses for us and the choices we made along those paths. We are survivors, we should feel pride in that and the strength we have shown ourselves to have."

"You write a lot about acceptance, Peter. As if it's the key to moving on. How do you find it?" I asked.

"Acceptance will find you," Peter assured me. "Your life has many surprises left for you. Trust that. When you're ready, get up and start seeking them out."

So, Enrico and I got up. Our cracks were pulled together like skin after a cut, still fragile but holding. Who I was, after what had been broken began to repair itself, was a different person. That was a truth I came to accept. The challenge became figuring out who that was. Being familiar with heartache means you know you will survive it. What you don't know is who you will be once you do.

"What do we do now?" I asked Enrico.

"I don't know," he replied. "We move on. Like we always have."

"After everything, would you still keep going?" I asked, conscious of all that question implied.

"I would. I would for you," he answered. "For us. We're stronger than this. I know you're struggling. I am too. But we move on. And we try again."

"We try again," I agreed. "What a tragic ending our story would have if we didn't. It simply can't end like this. Not like this."

"Then we won't let it," he said. And I believed him.

Peter spoke about acceptance as though it were a gate we had to walk through. I imagined it was made of burnished metal and that it would slam shut loudly once we passed through it. The banging sound a symbol of the outrage we would leave behind as we stepped through to the other side.

18 Count on Love

In the first picture I ever saw of him, he was crawling toward the camera as if he had something terribly important to say. His expression was serious and melancholic. I deleted the photo. In fact, I deleted the entire file.

Less than a week after the adoption fell through, a new file was sent to us from the agency in South Korea. They were proposing a new baby, a seven-month old boy. The problem was that Enrico and I weren't ready. Jumping from one baby to the next so quickly felt impossibly fast. There was no room within either of us for another tenuous promise. We refused the proposition. We said no.

Then we said maybe.

Adoption seems so random: with families and children straining to be connected, it's a numbers game, a waiting game that ends with your place in line matching theirs.

"I wonder if we need to think about this differently," Enrico said.

"What do you mean?"

"I think it would be a mistake to wait until we're ready. We're ready now."

Every effort I had made to forget the child's wistful face, failed. His eyes washed back into my mind pure as spring water, rinsing my eyes so I could see beyond the hurt. That was enough to bring me back. I retrieved his file from the trash on my computer, for the fourth or fifth time, and stared long and hard at his picture. I knew. Still side-stepping grief in my hallway, I curled up with Enrico on the couch.

"I think you're right. We should reconsider this baby," I said. "I can't stop thinking about him. I can't stop wanting him."

That's how it happened. Despite it all, we leapt once more. My husband wrapped his long arms around me. "I was thinking the same thing," he said. "I think he needs us. I've been opening and closing his file all day."

"So have I! It's like he's pulling me to him."

"That's how I feel too."

"We're doing this then?" I asked. "Really doing this?"

"Yes," Enrico answered. "You're the one who said our story doesn't have a tragic ending. Let's go find our happy one."

That precious baby had stirred something inside of us when we didn't believe we had the capacity to be moved. He did that, this faraway baby boy. It was he who chose us. We were simply awake enough to hear him. We used that stirring to unwrap what had been sheltered away, and reach out across oceans.

Within weeks, we started again down the long and winding road of adoption. This time though, we would do it quietly. With no fanfare, no pictures printed and framed on our walls. We filled out every paper and signed every document with cautious reserve. We did it all with slow, sedulous movements, afraid to believe, anxious about something else going wrong, frightened that one more blow would damage us beyond repair.

"Grief is an opportunity to explore your soul," Peter wrote. "Wade into what you're made of, Tarah, what you believe in and why you're alive."

I didn't want to give up on motherhood or myself. Enrico and I had come to understand that we had no choice but to be courageous. Wasn't our child, after all? He was a gift, and fear could not be what kept us from him. We needed to count on love, yet again, to bring us together. So that's what we did. We counted on love.

19 Up, Up and Away

A new baby meant another lengthy period of waiting. More uncomfortable months stretched out before us as the process ran its course. It was the stories that I lived and told that brought the greatest comfort.

We drove toward the airport in the middle of the night. The windows were open and a cool breeze slid across my face, waking me from sleep. The first glimpses of dawn appeared on the horizon, slivers of orange that seemed impatient to grow. The highway was deserted, a ribbon of grey asphalt before us with a bright yellow line leading the way. I leaned into the seat, a soft sweater pulled around my shoulders, my eyes as heavy as cream. Marc, the cameraman working with me that day, was sleepy as well. He held a steaming cup of coffee in one hand, the steering wheel in the other, the dreams of only a few hours earlier poking into the corners of his eyes like tiny fingers.

We passed the airport's departure gates and made our way toward a hangar the average traveller never sees. A Boeing 767 was stationed on the tarmac just outside enormous sliding doors. Marc parked the car, grabbed his camera equipment, and with our bags thrown over our shoulders, we carried everything we needed for the next twenty-four hours.

We heard the screaming and cheering long before we walked into the hangar. The excitement was like an invisible curtain. The joy, the exuberance felt so tangible, I imagined it left behind bits and pieces that clung to my hair. It shook the fatigue from my very bones. There were upwards of two hundred children inside, none of them able to contain the thrill that moved inside their bodies like laughter. Even those who used wheelchairs moved their arms in the air, stretching them to the sky, their heads bobbing up and down as if to music.

It was just after four in the morning.

The children were ushered outside, led up a metal staircase, and into the cabin of the plane. They were met by dozens of volunteers, including Air Canada flight attendants and pilots affiliated with a non-profit group called Dreams Take Flight. They were bringing a group of children, some with medical issues, others with difficult family situations to Walt Disney World for one day. One single day.

Once we were strapped into our seats, Captain Belanger, dressed in airline white with gold stripes across his shoulders, came over the intercom and asked a plane full of children to count down from ten.

"Here we go!" he yelled. "The plane can't move without you, so let's hear it!"

They began the countdown, loud and clear, giddy with excitement, and at *three...two...one...* the captain floored the gas pedal. The momentum pushed everyone back into their seats as the giant airliner roared down the runway and peeled into the sky.

"Woooohoooo!" they all yelled.

Most of these children, if not all, had never been on a plane before. They crowded by the windows and pulled at each other's elbows and shoulders as they tried to get a better view of what beckoned outside. When the sun finally rose, a stillness took over, a quiet that comes from watching a miracle happen right before your eyes.

There were so many children, but I was instantly drawn to a child named Alex. He was six years old, had cerebral palsy, and the most stunning hazel eyes I had ever seen. He used a wheelchair and did not speak. His guardian for the day was an airline captain in his mid-fifties, affectionately referred to as Captain Pierre. Alex may or may not have understood what was in store, but he clearly felt the energy around him. His eyes looked as if they were smiling.

"He's ready," said Captain Pierre. "I will make sure this is a day he will never forget."

"Why do you take part every year?" I asked Pierre. "What keeps bringing you back?"

"The children," he said.

"Is there a best part?" I asked him.

"Yes," he said, pulling Alex closer to him. "I'm determined to give him the best day possible, but I know, in the end, he will give me more. The best part is him."

We landed four hours after taking off, the energy around us pushed out in all directions like a balloon blown so thin it threatened to pop. The stories and magic within the world of Disney began to unfold: giant castles with stardust that glittered on window panes, white windmills that turned to the sound of bells, life-sized characters, rides that twirled in circles or floated up and down, and lane after lane fanning out like the petals of a daisy pointing toward more opportunities and adventures.

Marc and I found Alex riding Dumbo the elephant. He was sitting close to Captain Pierre, whose arms held him securely as the elephant floated ever higher into the air. The Captain spotted us and waved while Dumbo's ears tried to whisk them off to kinder lands. Alex's head bobbed back and forth, his hair flapping in the wind like wings.

"Look, Tarah!" shouted Captain Pierre. "Look at his eyes. It's all in his eyes!"

"I see!" I yelled back. "He looks so happy! And so do you!"

Beaming as they climbed off of the ride, Captain Pierre held Alex in his arms, his thin legs dangled like a doll's. Both of their faces were flushed pink with excitement.

"He's beautiful, isn't he?" said Captain Pierre.

"Yes, yes he is. He is beautiful," I said.

Captain Pierre squeezed him affectionately before placing him gently back into his wheelchair. Captain Pierre, who had four children of his own, had an infectious smile and he was so tender with Alex. What a loving father he must be, I thought.

"We're off to explore Cinderella's Castle," he said, pushing Alex's chair in the direction of the gilded mansion. "We have much to do and only one day to do it in!" The captain waved goodbye and his arm moved through the humid air.

"That was a pretty special moment," said Marc. He had filmed it all, captured what spilled between them, vital and pressing as a promise.

There were no medical appointments for the children that day. Struggling single parents or problems with money didn't find their way into that enchanted world. Instead, children rushed toward Space Mountain eager to throw the full weight of their delight into ships that would propel them through an unknown and starry universe. Others sought out fairies and fairy godmothers and the magical wands they carried.

I pointed out a little girl to Marc.

"The little blonde one?" he answered.

"Yes, let's go meet her," I said.

Her name was Rachel. She had lost one of her legs before her second birthday and now, at six, had suffered through several taxing surgeries. She was limping toward the entrance of It's a Small, Small World, pulling her artificial limb behind her, propelling herself forward as if she were trying to cross the finish line, chest first, with every stride. Her hair was the colour of lemon sherbet, her skin even paler. She seemed like an ethereal fairy skipping from one flower to the next, undaunted or unaware that what made her different also made her special.

"Are you coming with us?" she asked us, ponytail bobbing behind her, her T-shirt pink as bubble-gum.

"We'd like that very much," I answered. "Can we join you?"

She stepped toward me and wound her elfin fingers around mine and began chatting as if we had been lifelong friends.

"Did you know that fairies are real and that I spoke to one?" she asked. "It's a secret, but I'm sharing it with you."

"Thank you," I said. "I feel very lucky to have met you. What do fairies talk about?"

"All the good things, it's what they know."

We slipped into that Small World and onto tugboats that pulled us through colourful caves. Animals of all kinds and stars of all shapes loomed large before us.

"If you're worried about being trapped here," she said, "it's OK. It's where the magic happens."

"What kind of magic?" I asked her.

"The very best kind," she smiled, and left it at that. More secrets in that secret world.

"What has been your favourite place today?"

"Every place."

Her guardian laughed shyly. "She's a pretty special person," she told me. "I know she's young, but it's incredible to see how she never for one second lets anything stop her. No one has told her there's any reason she can't do it all. And so she does."

Almost twenty hours after we had taken off from Montreal, hours of footage and interviews later, we turned for home. The children piled back into the plane, their smiling faces dirty with chocolate, sweat, and cotton candy. I was certain they had found the magic they searched for, magic they smuggled back, tucked into the pockets of their shorts or held firmly in their fists. Day had turned to night once more and our plane moved through the clouds, the wind whispering bedtime stories as 200 pairs of eyes closed.

Rachel was curled up in her seat airy as an angel about to drop to earth. Alex too, was fast asleep, Captain Pierre in the seat beside him, ever watchful. Mops of hair swept into closed eyes, sugar stains grew crusty on T-shirts, running shoes were strewn around the plane like pebbles at the bottom of a dried-out lake. The sounds of breathing grew heavier, moving in unison like an orchestra. Marc turned off the camera and we both sat to watch the city drift into view. We would land soon.

"I'm so tired," Marc said.

"Me too. I'm exhausted." I answered. "It was a good day though, wasn't it?"

"Very," He agreed. "You have a lot of footage to go through to tell this story."

"I'm not worried. Something tells me it will tell itself."

Marc and I drove back home along the same road we had come by twenty-four hours earlier. We hardly spoke, craving the escape of our beds. It took two days for the story to be screened, written and edited, two days to recreate our vision of such an extraordinary day. It remains one of my favourite pieces.

There are so many moments that remain vivid in my mind: Alex's eyes, Captain Pierre's enthusiasm, Rachel's inviting and eager explanations. Along with the memories, the lessons have stayed with me. There were many: ones of strength and perseverance. And courage. The kind of courage that feels intuitive to the young. No matter what life places before them, they survive and cultivate a warrior's strength. I wonder if this many years later, they live their lives with the same singular passion they did that day. If they can remember how they were afraid of nothing and open to everything. It is my hope for them. It is my wish upon a star.

20 Clinging to Hope

Eight.

Interminable.

Months.

That's how long it took before the adoption agency contacted us again. The waiting was filled with crushing silences, wearisome moments, nights that stretched on endlessly, days that wouldn't dawn, microwaves that didn't ding, food that wouldn't arrive, grass that didn't grow. It was all of that rolled into one gigantic pause that confined us in place. We were unable to move forward, desperate for one phone call that would set us free.

And then it came.

"Book your tickets," said Tina, our case worker. "It's time to meet your son."

Unfortunately, her phone call also came with some caveats. South Korea's adoption rules and protocols had changed, becoming stricter, more demanding. Had the first adoption worked out, we would have been the final family in before the changes were implemented. As it stood now, we were the first of three Canadian families (all from Quebec) adopting children under these new regulations. We would all arrive in Seoul at the same time and forge an instant and, in one case, a lifelong bond that comes from living something so unique together. Enrico and I listened to our case worker, frustrated, shaking our heads at how yet another obstacle was lodged in our path.

"What do we have to do?" I asked Tina. "Tell us what we have to do, and we'll do it."

"Get on a plane as soon as you can," she said. "Once you're there, everything will be made clear. The first step is to go."

Within days, I temporarily left my position at the television station and Enrico put his clients on hold. Our family and friends hugged us tightly good-bye. My brother, who had been living in China for more than a decade, wished us Man Zou—a Mandarin farewell that translates roughly into "walk slowly." Walk slowly and you will not fall.

The night before we left for Seoul my sister and mother held me in their arms and whispered prayers of encouragement. We all wanted to believe that everything would work out, the believing was the important part.

"Are you ready?" Enrico asked in the taxi to the airport.

"Holding my breath, I guess. What about you?"

"This is further than we've ever made it before," he said. "This time it will work."

"I know," I said. "What could possibly go wrong?" He smiled. An understanding lived between us.

"I can't believe we're on our way to meet him," he said. "That it's really happening."

Two planes, 10,500 kilometres, and almost a day later, we arrived in South Korea.

"Welcome to Seoul," said Hyeyoung, our adoption case worker. Hyeyoung would come to mean a great deal to me, and after a very long journey that had yet to be walked, would be instrumental in helping me find my way home. But neither of us at the moment could have imagined what lay ahead.

"Are you ready to meet your son?" she asked.

"Very, very ready," we told her.

"I have booked an appointment for two days from now," she said. "But until then we have much to discuss."

Hyeyoung explained that despite all the paperwork, background checks, references, and the enormity of our file, a youth court judge we would meet only once had the power to refuse our request to be parents. There was no precedent, no way to know if this was just a formality or if, as the first families through this new adoption maze, the stricter rules meant fewer approvals. Like many nations, South Korea was trying to limit international adoption, but the greater truth was there were too many children born needing families than the country could ever house themselves.

"Do you think we should be concerned?" I asked her. "Could something go wrong?"

"I'm sure everything will be just fine."

"How quickly can we take him home once we've gone before the judge," I asked.

"Oh, Tarah," she said. "At least a month."

"That's so long," I sighed. When what I really wanted to say was, *A MONTH! AN ENTIRE MONTH?*

She looked at me kindly. "I know it is, but maybe it will go faster."

The reasons were bureaucratic. Papers needed to be translated and departing visas needed to arrive. But all I kept thinking was that it was one more month our baby would be growing up without us.

From the time Enrico and I had decided we wanted to have a child, almost six long years had passed. We hoped that these were going to be our final steps, that we had lived through our share of hurts, that we would finally be rewarded for our patience and perseverance.

We hoped. It was really all we had, so we held onto it for dear life.

21 For You We Crossed the World

Seoul was like a black and white watercolour painting that had been left out in the rain. Water droplets streamed down the car's windows, and the faster we drove, the more the city looked washed-out and grey. We had been in the van for more than half an hour, Hyeyoung in front and Enrico and I in back, and still there was building after building crowding the sides of the highway, giant apartment complexes with huge number signs on rooftops: 223, 224, 225. And on and on it went. One of the most populous countries in the world per land mass needed an extraordinary number of homes.

"It's incredible how big the city is," Enrico said. "So many people."

"Almost 10 million. And amid all these millions of people…" I replied. "It still doesn't seem real."

"Are you OK?" he asked.

"I am," I answered. "A bit nervous. That first moment, you know?"

"After so long. There's finally a first moment."

We stopped somewhere in the three hundreds and made our way to the second floor, then down a hallway to a door at the end of a corridor. It was painted a vivid yellow with discoloured grey patches near the doorknob where the pigment had chipped away. There was a well-used playground down below we could see from the hallway, which was open and exposed to the outside. I wondered how cold the city would be in winter. Shoes were placed tidily outside every door. Red and blue toddler bikes leaned sleepily against concrete walls.

"Are you ready?" Hyeyoung asked.

"We are," I said.

She knocked.

"You must see so many of these moments, people meeting their child for the first time."

"I do," she beamed. "And every one is special."

The woman who answered the door had short, straight hair and wore thin wire-frame glasses. She spoke quickly to Hyeyoung then ushered us into her home. Her name was Soo and she was our child's foster parent. She had been caring for him for six months. Soo pointed to a low table surrounded by cushions on the floor in the centre of her small living room. She urged us to sit then returned to the kitchen where she busied herself preparing plates of sweet mango.

Enrico and I sat nervously, almost uncomfortably. We looked around the apartment, knowing our son was somewhere close by. Hyeyoung disappeared briefly into an adjacent room and when she returned, she had our child in her arms.

"Here he is," whispered Hyeyoung. "Here's your baby."

She walked over to the table where we were sitting and gently placed him on the ground. He was just over a year old and stood firmly on his two feet.

Everything around me felt more in focus. We were staring at our son. *This is our son.* I felt elated, overflowing with emotion. I could hear my heart beating, it pounded so furiously.

Our baby boy stared at us with the same gaze that looked out from the photos we had stashed in our wallets. He had on a blue-and-white striped T-shirt and his baby-soft hair dropped down into one eye. Nobody moved. I didn't know if I should touch him or hold him. He was surreal, beautiful, divine, perfect.

I heard Hyeyoung giggle as our child's foster mother scooped up the baby and placed him gently in Enrico's lap.

"She says it's OK to hold him," said Hyeyoung, "Don't be afraid. He's your child."

Enrico was trying to be calm, but I could tell he was nervous. More nervous, I imagined, than this baby who looked up at him with beautiful brown eyes. He reached up to rub his tiny nose and then opened his mouth as though to ask Enrico a question, but nothing came out.

I was stifling the urge to pull him into my arms and cover him with kisses, telling myself to breathe. We would have a life together if only I was patient a while longer. This is the thought I embraced first, not much different from a new mother when she holds a newborn baby in her arms.

Over the course of one hour we fed him fruits, and watched him play. His foster mother put on music and encouraged him to dance. We all laughed as he stomped around and spun in circles. We were witnesses to what could be, but still far removed from the family I wanted us to be. I didn't stop smiling for a single second.

All too soon, it was over.

"I'm sorry, but we must go now," Hyeyoung announced.

"Already?"

"I know it hasn't been long," she said, "but you'll see him again soon. OK?"

"Can I hug him goodbye?" I asked her.

"Of course!" she exclaimed. "He is your son."

I drew his body to mine. He looked up at me questioningly. "Soon," I promised, and I touched his face which was unimaginably soft. I inhaled his baby scent, so clean and new. I closed my eyes, wanting to remember the feeling of him in my arms before I let him go.

As we left Soo's home, I wanted to rewind and relive some of those precious minutes. I wanted to stay and memorize every curve in his face, every expression, every movement. I wanted to take him in my arms and never let him go. I wanted my baby with me. To leave him felt like something inside me ripping.

Instead, what we took away was only a taste of what could be, a glimpse of who he could become to us. For now, he would stay with the woman he knew as his mother. The title might be mine on paper, but it would take time for me—and for him—to feel it in the way that mattered.

Change whispered in the wind as we walked through the rain. "Tell me how you're feeling," I asked Enrico, on the long ride back to our hotel.

"It's strange," he said. "It's still sinking in. I just want everything from this moment on, to go smoothly."

"I know," I said. "But we're here now, and we've met him. Everything will be OK."

We saw him again two days later, this time in the playroom of Seoul's adoption agency, and again we had one short hour. This time we were left alone with him. I touched him, held him close, inhaled the smell of his hair, and felt his skin against mine. He had such dreamy eyes and they looked straight into mine. He was a happy child, cared for. He had no idea that his entire world had been logged and organized, preparing him for a future far away.

It gutted me to say goodbye. I wanted to feel like his mother. Instead, I watched him climb into Soo's arms, his play date with two strangers over. He was going back to his life, and we were going to stand before a judge. As Enrico and I left the agency, we felt heavy with hope and fear.

I said a silent prayer that I would see him again. That he would truly become ours. I couldn't speak because it felt as though my heart was climbing up my throat, ready to throw itself out of my body in order to stay behind. I swallowed to push it back down. I held onto Enrico and looked back only once.

22 The Judge

As a reporter, I have covered many kinds of court stories. I have sat among my peers with our notepads and pens, watched as lawyers draped in ebony gowns defended their clients and prosecutors pushed for jail time. I have watched accused murderers sit expressionless behind the thick glass of the defender's box, their shoulders hunched, their wrists restrained by metal cuffs, their eyes down.

Court stories are not easy to tell when you work in television. Reporters are allowed into Canadian courtrooms, but not camera people or photographers. They are corralled behind thick, yellow lines and scramble into action when the proceedings are adjourned. Together we catch lawyers speeding back to their offices like blackbirds, their long robes fluttering behind them. On occasion they will stop for a throng of reporters, flash bulbs lighting up the whites of their eyes.

I have watched mourning or outraged families sitting in icy courtroom pews. During the trial of a young Quebec man accused of killing a three-year-old girl, the courtroom was packed with families demanding justice or begging for mercy. The crash that had killed the child happened on the accused's 18th birthday, when he took his father's car keys and went for a drive, despite having only a learner's permit. Driving too fast in a residential area, the young man bent to answer his cell phone, veered off the road and hit a young girl who was playing outside her house. His lawyer argued it had been an accident.

The young man sat in the courtroom, pale and quiet. His family forlorn for the life their son had taken and for his own, which was now forever changed. The family of the girl was enraged; they wanted the eighteen-year-old thrown behind bars. There could be no winners, only an opportunity for the justice system to do its best to dole out punishment. In the end, the young man was sentenced to two years less a day with a host of conditions, including house arrest for the first year. Many people felt the sentence was not harsh enough. How do you measure how someone pays for taking a life? What is it worth?

In South Korea I prepared to stand before a judge, in my own defence, for the first time. Enrico and I were one of many couples who paced vanilla-coloured corridors dressed in our nicest outfits, stealing glances at others who had also come to plead their case. On the street outside the courthouse we finally met the two other Quebec families adopting babies. We smiled and asked each other questions, feeling a kind of comfort in the shared anxiety of what the day would decide. After everything it had taken to get to this point, so much rested on what one person thought of us. How could we tell someone we had never met that we were deserving?

Finally, the doors to the courtroom opened and a woman called our names. She escorted us into a large, dimly lit room with beige carpeting. The judge's bench was empty, but in front of the imposing wood bench was a small round glass table, the kind you would find in an office. There were no pews for visitors, just one other small desk against the back wall of the room where a woman in a pale flowered dress was writing in a notepad. Two men were sitting at the glass table. One of them stood, signalled for us to take the two empty chairs and introduced himself as our translator. His English was barely passable! *How can this be our translator?* I felt my blood pressure begin to rise.

The other man was the judge. Tall and thin, wearing a suit far too big for him, he asked us about our backgrounds, our lives and our families. We answered as well as we could, careful to not overwhelm the translator with too many details or difficult words. I wanted to tell the judge everything— every wish, every struggle, every moment, every decision I had ever made that had led me here, to this place. I wanted to tell him that I would nurture, support, care for and encourage this child to be everything he could possibly be. I would be there when he fell, to tell him that falling is OK, because it shows us that we can get up. That we can be brave. I would hold him when he needed me to and when he faced hard things, I would be there. Always, forever.

How do you say all that?

I couldn't. So, I showed him what I did have. The precious moments that had made up our beginning. Our life-altering beginning.

I quickly set up a series of photos on my tablet, images from the two visits that had been filled with laughter, tenderness, affection, and wonder. There were about a dozen, each telling the story of a possible future. I watched the judge look at each and every one. Enrico and I sat close together and I knew, as a smile pulled across the judge's face and stayed there, that we had shown him what this child's life would be filled with. Without words, he saw that this baby was already ours.

He asked no more questions, but said something to the translator and then turned to us. The translator seemed to be choosing his words carefully, as if he was picturing them in his mind, lining them up like train cars so that they would tumble out in the right order.

"He approves your adoption," he said. "He asks only one thing."

"Anything," we both answered. "What does he want?"

"He asks that you give him a good education."

I turned to the judge, my eyes wet.

"Will you tell him something for me?" I asked the translator. "Tell him I promise that his education will be a priority. That he will learn about his history and his culture. Tell him that he will always know love."

I watched the judge's thin face. He nodded.

I wanted to hug him in his oversized blue suit, but I held back. I reached out my hand and he held it for a quick moment. He had many other families to attend to that day.

23 Homesick for the You I Dreamed Of

On the wide streets of Seoul, where three-lane highways expanded into spacious sidewalks, where pedestrians walked under tunnels to cross to the other side of the street, where boutiques, cafes and storefront windows beckoned, there was art. Giant sculptures made of various metals or massive stones appeared next to buildings or beside windows. They were so unobtrusive in the city's landscape, you might walk right by them, not realizing that they are worth stopping for.

Enrico and I were fascinated by these unique sculptures and found every opportunity to seek them out. It became a kind of game we played during our final days in Seoul. Some were whimsical: like a giant bucket, made entirely out of metal, that poured out a rich grey liquid that pooled on the sidewalk. Or a ten-foot bird with clouds bursting from its body and wings, trying to take flight from a concrete perch. I found myself thinking about these sculptures as examples of what you do not see unless you are looking.

We played carefree tourists. Museums are plentiful and free, and there were often English translations of exhibits. In the War Memorial of Korea, a group of young children, perhaps four- or five-year olds, gathered around my tall, white husband, giggling and pointing up at him. He was an anomaly to them. In that same museum we learned about South Korea's history and how close the country came to annihilation after North Korea, backed by the Soviet Union and China, invaded at the start of the Korean War in the early 1950s.

We also learned how important bloodlines are in South Korea. It comes from the pain of the past.

Because so many children were put up for adoption after the Korean War, in 2012, for the first time in its history, the country's adoption rules were changed to reduce the number of Korean children being adopted abroad. The new rules were created to add what leaders called accountability to the process. The rules required new mothers wait at least five days before relinquishing their child to the state, and that no international adoptions would be allowed before a baby turned five months old. Each child put up for adoption was also registered to ensure a child would be able to track down the biological parents. But in South Korea, pregnancy outside of marriage is frowned upon, and there is a social stigma, which is why baby boxes, actual boxes where frightened mothers place their children before fleeing without a word, are still used. Baby boxes have histories in multiple countries around the world and they will likely continue to be used until pregnant women are properly supported and can safely come forward without consequences. Children left in baby boxes are not considered for international adoption.

For the women who do legally give up their babies, the gratitude of mothers like me can never be overstated. I want to hold their hands in mine and promise that their gift of life is more welcome than they could ever imagine. A gift so precious, it could bring a fossilized heart back to life.

No longer having time with our son meant neither of us felt the need to stay in South Korea. Hyeyoung had said it would take at least one month for the court's judgement to be translated into English and for a visa to be issued. We needed a Canadian Permanent Residency Visa which would give our baby immediate residency status once he landed in Canada. No Korean child would be allowed out of the country without it.

Enrico would fly back to Montreal from Seoul, while I headed south to Thailand, which was more affordable. Staying in South Korea was financially impossible for us, and I had already decided that I wouldn't leave this part of the world without our baby.

We parted ways with the two other Quebec families, who were also heading back to Montreal, promising to stay in touch as the process ran its course. We needed one another's support and understanding. It made us all feel less alone. Muriel and Gilbert, who had adopted a baby boy from South Korea five years earlier, were eagerly awaiting their second son. We had met ten thousand kilometres from Montreal but realized we lived only ten minutes from each other. I hugged them good-bye, promising to write the moment I landed back in Seoul.

At Seoul's Incheon Airport, composed of a sprawling and bustling series of buildings, Enrico and I held onto each other like leaves in a windstorm. As passengers rushed past us to find boarding gates and catch planes, we stood still. Airports feel as if they are constantly moving, like the magical staircases in Harry Potter that bring you someplace new and strange. There is rarely any uncertainty in the energy of those who travel; they know exactly where they want to go.

With overstuffed carry-on bags and horseshoe-shaped pillows, travellers sipped steaming cups of coffee and plunked down in airport lounge areas, their bodies crumpling. Outside the floor-to-ceiling windows, planes landed and took off, a seemingly never-ending game of "Where is it going?" I held my husband, my head pushed into his chest, somehow afraid that when I let him go life would drop another obstacle in front of us, making the way back to him shrouded.

"I love you," I said. "I'll be home in just over a month. With our baby."

Enrico said he left that day with the image that I would be delivering our child to us. Not in the way most mothers do, from their bodies, but from halfway around the world strapped tightly to my chest. We held each other as long as we could before we separated and stepped in to join the crowds of moving people. We were pulled apart like cars turning into traffic. He went one way and I the other. I lost sight of him quickly, as people filled the wide hallway and blocked my view.

Faith

24 Blessed With Luck

The temples in Thailand push up from the earth like hands in prayer. They are covered with thousands of coloured ceramic squares that glitter playfully. Giant golden Buddhas offer from their chipped fingers the teachings of kindness, compassion, and equanimity. On Koh Samui, a Thai island where I waited for news about our son, there were dozens of temples, some large and ornate, others smaller and more reserved. It's where I spent a month learning about Buddhism.

Buddhism is the official religion of Thailand and temples play an important role. A wat is a type of Buddhist temple that is beyond a place of worship. They include areas for prayer, learning, sleeping and eating. It's where monks live and meditate, and tourists are often granted entry to enjoy the silence, explore the grounds or marvel at the magnificent old Buddha statues. I loved exploring these calming places. I loved crossing paths with the monks who seemed so gentle and wise. In the early mornings I heard the chanting that drifted out from nearby wats and filled the air.

The first wat I visited was the island's largest. To enter I passed under a gilded, steep roof where serpents looked down menacingly. The grounds were large and spread out but there were no signs to point the way. The earth was dry and dusty from the unrelenting sun. Directly in front of me was a simple shelter with wooden floorboards and a thatched roof, so I walked toward it needing to escape the heat. I removed my shoes and, stepping quietly, placed each foot carefully. Old, dusty images of the Buddha on yellowing paper with crumpled edges were cluttered in a central display. Incense burned, filling the air with the strong smells of wood and flowers, the smoke staying as if by choice, even without walls to contain it.

I walked toward six stately Buddha statues, some with ears or noses broken off, but they seemed a happy welcoming committee in spite of these imperfections. They were open to the elements and showed clear signs of how long they had been standing; the gold stain that once covered them had rubbed off, leaving a muddy brown in its place. At the base of each Buddha were ripples of dried wax pooled like sand on the floor. I stood in silence and prayed for patience.

From there I moved farther into the complex and saw long wooden tables that looked like an outdoor dining area. Monks sat and sipped what I assumed were mugs of tea. It seemed like I had entered a more private living space within the wat grounds where fewer tourists wandered, but no one told me I was intruding so I continued on. The living area was covered with a large tarp which provided shade. A square mirror had been hung on a thick wooden post and I saw a monk peering into it to shave his head. He saw me watching him, and smiled through the glass. I glanced down as if I had been caught witnessing a moment that was his alone. I walked, conscious of each print my bare feet made in the earth, the welcome weight of past prayer around me. A calm floating up from the ground. Saffron-coloured robes hung on a line drying in the midday sun. Drawn to the sounds of rippling water I found a river and a skinny kitten curled up by its banks sleeping in the blue plastic head of a dirty shovel. I bent down to stroke its fur, its purring sounded like distant thunder.

Closer to the main entrance, where my sandals still baked in the sun, was a large covered resting area with places to sit. An older monk sat on an elevated wooden platform, his burgundy robes spilling around him. He had skin the colour of bronze and large eyes. He caught my gaze and held it. He pointed to the space in front of him and invited me to claim it. He held a bunch of dried reeds tied together with twine, and beside him was a bucket of water. He pointed to it and, in strongly accented English, said, "For luck."

I was in Thailand to work on building faith and conquering fear and was certainly open to some luck. I sat before him on a thin blue cushion with my palms together against my chest, and he began to chant. The sound was guttural. He dipped the reeds into the bucket and, while he sang, the most glorious cold water droplets rained down upon me. Thailand is sweltering in July. In the heated haze, filled with hot incense, that cold prayer shower was in itself a gift. The two minutes I sat there were magical and healing. I had been blessed with luck.

With his prayer complete, the monk stopped chanting. When I opened my eyes, he was tying strings together. He twisted threads of bright orange, yellow and green into a woven bracelet. He took my wrist in his cool and calloused hands and tied the threads so they wouldn't fall off.

"For luck," he said to me again, nodding sharply.

"Khob-kun-ka," I answered back. Thank you.

25 Under the Sitting Tree

My home for the month was a bungalow across the street from the ocean. It was a single, stand-alone room with a bed, a dresser and a washroom. The windows were open but covered by much-needed screens and the roof was high with a light that dropped down from a black wire. The main hotel was ocean-front and by those sandy beaches was where I ate my breakfast of fresh fruit and spent many hours of my day. A group of three enchanting old trees stood on that beach. Huge, thick trunks had clawed their way out of the sand and grown tall and powerful. The branches, a rich earthy brown, were full and stretched out in all directions. The jade green leaves were wide and made music when the wind blew.

While most hotels on that stretch of sand had umbrellas to offer shade, we had these trees. I called the one I sat under every day the sitting tree. It was the biggest and most imposing of the trio, with branches that reached toward the ocean.

All day long women and men walked the beach, selling colourful sarongs and dresses, clay pots and souvenirs to visitors and hotel guests. Others carried giant pieces of wood draped with beaded necklaces and bracelets that hung down, jingling and jangling with every step. They sold water and blended drinks, carried portable stoves for grilling ears of corn or pieces of meat. Fruit sellers chopped sweet, fleshy mangos and ripe melons, which they offered in clear plastic bags with toothpicks. There was a never-ending demand for these bags of fruit.

As the vendors walked up and down the beach they often stopped to sit under the tree and its delicious patch of shade. They laughed with one another while escaping the heat of the day. It made me happy, seeing them under the sitting tree. They congregated and chatted away, and though I had no idea what they were saying, it was musical and full of happy tones. They then moved on, only to return after another long, scorching walk.

The sellers, who spent their days under the sun, took great care to cover their skin. Most wore wide-brimmed hats in pinks and yellows. Under those straw hats, they wrapped thin, cotton towels around their faces and necks, so in some cases all you saw were a pair of watchful eyes and a nose. Long sleeves covered their arms, and fingerless gloves hid their hands. Most wore long, loose pants that billowed like drapes near an open window. On their sandalled feet were old white socks turned a dingy caramel from the dust.

Only while we were all under the sitting tree did I see their faces. The expanse of the tree was so vast, that fifteen to twenty people were easily shaded under its branches. The men were less worried about covering up, but the women took it very seriously. After several days they'd gotten used to my presence and didn't try to sell me anything anymore.

It was Satyia who first told me she wanted to keep her skin as white as possible. Satyia was a young woman who worked at the hotel; she left towels and water in my bungalow and changed the sheets once a week. Some days, feeling homesick, I curled up in my room and hid from the wide, hot world outside it. On one of those afternoons, Satyia found me, and, without hesitation, started chatting, making herself comfortable on the bed beside me, sitting cross-legged as if we were lifelong friends catching up on our lives. I hadn't had a lot of human contact since leaving Enrico at the airport, so her camaraderie was as charming as it was soothing.

"Beautiful," said Satyia, touching me gently. "So... pale."

Touching her own arm, and without looking up, said, "Not!"

"No, very beautiful," I said. "You are lovely!"

She shook her head fiercely. "Everyone says white is better."

"They are wrong," I told her, seriously.

I took her hands in mine. They were the rough hands of a woman who had scrubbed and cleaned for most of her life. Her skin was tanned, a deep, rich brown. My Irish heritage means my skin is pale, and like so many Westerners I've been drawn to the image of a glowing tan as something beautiful to strive for. Every culture has its stereotypes of beauty standards, especially for women, and Satyia saw her complexion only as a sign of her status in life.

"Dark is bad in Thailand," she said. "We work and we work, and we grow dark."

"You are very beautiful," I said.

I wanted her to see her own beauty, but she shrugged off my compliments.

She explained that she had been paler as a child, and that her skin had grown darker because she worked outside. She would never have considered spending her meager income on something as frivolous as sunscreen, and it probably wouldn't have made that much difference. Her skin gave her away as a low-income worker, she said.

When I ran out of face moisturizer, I was surprised how difficult it was to find a single product that didn't include "whitening". I began noticing that women staring out from giant billboards were extremely pale. Advertisements of women and men framed in bus stops, staring out from magazines, on TV, in films, were as fair skinned as possible.

All these images are reinforcing a dangerous and misleading ideal that made people like Satyia feel inferior because of the colour of her skin.

Satyia helped me cultivate a new level of compassion for the young women who kept all but their eyes shaded. Under the thick branches and wide leaves of the sitting tree, I watched them in a new way.

"Satyia," I yelled, when I saw her walking from my bungalow after a day by the beach. "Come have tea with me!"

"OK, Ta-rah," she said. "I come to sit. You make tea, you bring cookies."

"Deal!" I laughed.

She was the closest person I had to a friend so far from home.

26 A Thousand Words

At dusk, the ocean was still and quiet, almost empty of people. The bright yellow of the day faded back to dusty blue. The sky had a pink hue, and the clouds once white and full turned to wads of cotton candy.

There were just a few stragglers. A guitar player plucking strings, the occasional swimmer, dirty dogs lying quietly by tossed-aside chairs. I could have stayed in that place forever.

"I miss you."

"I miss you too."

It had been more than a week since I had seen Enrico's face or heard his voice. The internet was finicky, and we never knew how long a video chat would last. To have any hope of reaching home there was one small section of the hotel, right outside the lobby entrance, where the internet was strongest. But even there, as I sat uncomfortably on the stone step with my tablet, I could never be sure a connection would be made. Some days we had minutes, others seconds, but rarely longer than that. Long enough to take a few tender words and hold them close.

"Any news?" he asked.

"Nothing yet, but my plan hasn't changed. I'm booked to fly out at the end of the month."

"How are you passing your days?"

"Pretty blissfully," I told him. "My days are slow, and I spend most of them by the water or in the wats."

We wrote to each other often, that was how we communicated. My days were his nights, so I woke up to caring notes and fell asleep sending them. We tested out names for our son, discarding many, putting others into a "maybe" file, tweaking and reducing the number of choices. His birth name was Geon, which we would always keep as part of his heritage, but we ruminated on what name felt right to us. As his parents. Now that we had met him. Now that we would love him for life.

"So we're agreed?" he asked. "Samuel?"

"I think it's perfect," I said. "Sam."

We had a child and had given him a name, yet we were still separated in three countries, thousands of kilometres apart. Adoption takes such a toll. You persevere, you hope, you wait. Waiting never did get any easier.

"Not right, Ta-rah," she said. "Babies stay with their mothers!"

Satyia's reaction to Sam required patience and understanding. She always had a ton of questions for me when she happily caught me in my bungalow.

"Why no husband?" she asked me.

"I have a husband. He is back at our home," I explained. "Soon I will be there too, with our baby."

"No belly, no baby," she said.

"Not always," I smiled.

Satyia had a three-year-old daughter and couldn't comprehend the concept of adoption. Her life had not been easy. She had become pregnant young and was raising her child with her mother's help. She found it outrageous that someone would give away their baby.

"Some mothers can't care for their children, Satyia," I said. "So they give their babies to someone who can."

"No. No. No," She insisted. "Babies and mothers stay together."

"But what if there are too many babies and not enough mothers who can care for them?" I asked her. "I could care for one."

"So you have one," she said.

"I tried," I explained. "But even if I could, it takes true strength to let a baby go. It is a gift. For me. For the baby."

Her face, usually so open and happy, turned angry, her thick brows furrowed, pulling together and pointing downward like caterpillars off for a march. I could almost see her thoughts pushing back behind her eyes.

"Not sure," she said. "Not sure, Ta-rah."

With that she turned, her arms full of sheets, and walked out the door.

I felt that was progress.

27 The Company of Strange Creatures

I shared my bungalow with geckos. Furtive creatures, brown or olive green, similar to lizards. They can stay frozen on a wall for hours, not moving a muscle, as if hoping their hushed existence will buy them safe passage through the night. They eat bugs, which I enthusiastically approved of. I adored having them in my room and found myself scanning the walls for geckos, eager for their quiet company. They were like tiny allies sharing my space.

When I was younger, my dear friend Miranda used to have nightmares about snakes strangling her. Miranda and I lived in the same city for only one year, but it was an important year. We were in our early twenties, and adulthood was staring us both in the face. We were ready to embrace womanhood yet still felt like girls playing dress-up.

When Miranda left Montreal, we became pen pals, and though we've only seen each other a dozen or so times over the years, I still consider her a close friend, a kind of spiritual sister. We often seek each other out during challenging periods, and pick up as if we've been in touch two days ago instead of two years. I tell her she's akin to my journal—someone I write to share ideas with, send stories to when I don't want words hidden away in books that will end up at the back of a closed drawer.

Miranda was a close companion on my entire journey through Asia. An email from her was like candy consumed hungrily. She's the one who recommended the novel I was reading, *Shantaram,* and I curled up with it every day under the sitting tree.

After my early morning yoga classes, I often dozed by the ocean and fell asleep watching the world of our beach move by like driftwood. One sticky afternoon, I noticed a family walking nearby, a German couple with one son aged about fifteen. I wondered what Enrico and I would be like as parents, what we would be like as a family.

I smiled when the family noticed the sitting tree and stopped. They spread out their towels and lay down under the shade of those redemptive leaves. They were quiet and kind with one another. People-watching was a way to connect with others in a land very far from my own.

I felt the pull of sleep, but just as my eyes closed, I felt a profound desire to open them again. The father and his son were at the foot of my sunbed, so close I could see their chests rise and fall as they breathed, as if they had just come back from a run and had something important to tell me. Both had wide, blue eyes, filled with what I thought may have been panic, but in my drowsy state I couldn't be sure. The father stretched his long arm toward me. It was a strange moment. We had not exchanged a single word, and I wasn't exactly sure what to do.

The father made the next move, taking a slow, calculated step closer to me. He leaned in, his arm taut, muscles clenched, encouraging me again, to reach for him. I saw him swallow, and when he opened his mouth, in broken English, he said one word: "Snake."

He was suddenly clear and real and relevant. Looking straight into my eyes, he whispered one more word. "Slowly."

That's when the adrenaline kicked in. In one quick movement, I grabbed at him, felt our palms touch, and screamed. He pulled with considerable force and I went flying out of my chair, landing in the sand, where I wiped at my body frantically, in case the snake had grabbed hold and flown along with me.

We pulled my belongings away and found the snake under the cushion of my chair, curled around the wooden bars of the bed as if it would have been content to take a long nap right along with me. It was shooed away, and all four feet slithered, first into some tall grass, and then up and away into the safety of the sitting tree.

I thanked my German saviours profusely, and we all laughed. They barely spoke English and I was extremely grateful that the word snake happened to be in their limited vocabulary. They then continued on down the beach.

I walked back to my bungalow where I was greeted by butterflies. They fluttered around as if telling me silent stories of what they had seen on their journeys. Today I had a story for them.

28 Dusk

"Let me help you, Ta-rah," said Satyia.

She had poked her head in through my window as I pulled my hair up into a bun.

"Going out?" she asked.

"Just to find some dinner," I told her.

She was soon running her fingers through my hair, expertly braiding pieces and pinning it all up so that my neck was free.

"There," she encouraged, "now you're ready."

"Do you like living on the island?" I asked her.

"I know nothing else," she answered. "I think so. But I will never leave here, so I must like it."

"And what about your daughter? When she grows up, will she stay here with you?"

She fussed with the final, rebellious strands and stayed quiet for a few minutes.

"I want her to take a plane, to see the world," she said. "To see it for me too. Now go before it gets too late."

At dusk, the island began its transformation. Darkness descended on dry, dusty streets, masking what daylight made visible: uneven roofs, dilapidated buildings, trash blown into alleyway corners. Mango sellers were replaced by travelling, makeshift crepe burners with young Indian chefs who offered chocolate delicacies for just a few dollars. Thick smoke billowed out from the exhaust pipes of the scooters that took over the streets. Slow-moving tourists wore their burned shoulders with pride.

Stores kept their doors thrown wide open and music blared from loudspeakers hanging from the ceiling. Hosts dressed in crisp, white shirts competed for attention as fresh fish lay on cold beds of ice. Hungry dogs and cats skulked in the shadows, hoping for scraps, while laughter and loud voices filled the air, humid with the day's heat. The island was ready for the night ahead.

Sauntering through the congested streets in tight, beaded dresses with long feathers, a dozen cabaret performers flirted and stuffed pamphlets into sweaty palms for their popular twice-nightly shows.

"Come inside, pretty lady!" they cajoled every evening. "Come hear us sing!"

They wore impressive costumes and had impeccably applied makeup and surreal bodies. They were gorgeous and they knew it, puckering their carefully lined lips, thrusting their breasts toward smiling tourists as flash bulbs snapped and crackled. For a few extra dollars you could wrap your arms around their slender waists to document the moment with photos. The performers were experts at lip-syncing, and their shows were a big attraction. I spent a few nights there myself, curled up on a red velvet sofa enjoying the air conditioning, a sweet drink and sing-along hits from the eighties.

Satyia giggled when I told her about the shows.

"I could never!"

We sat on my front step, Satyia's cleaning cart was off to the side filled with water and tiny shampoo bottles.

"Does your daughter know her father?" I asked.

"No, he isn't here," she said. "He isn't with us."

"You were very young when you became a mother."

She looked at me. "Too young. But that is life. I had no choice when I became with child."

"Do you have a choice where you come from?" she asked.

"We do. And so should all women."

"Maybe one day," she shrugged. "Maybe my daughter will know a different world."

"I hope she does."

"Can I come in for tea, Ta-rah?" she asked.

"Yes," I smiled at her. "I'll get some. Make yourself at home."

29 From the Hands of the Dalai Lama

There was a door-shaped space cut into the thick concrete. A well-worn mat lay before the entrance where shoes were left. It was damp inside, almost wet. The only light came from two small windows. Dust particles floated and danced in that light. Cobwebs draped from one end of the room to the other, the slightest touch sending insects scampering away into shadowy corners. Statues of the Buddha filled almost every inch of the space, some lying down, others sitting, big ones, small ones, each draped in a gold-coloured sarong with bits of dried flowers hanging around their necks. Despite their many faces and expressions, it was the stillest place in which I had ever set foot.

I found this old wat because of my brother. He had been to Thailand before and encouraged me to find it. It was tucked behind unidentified streets, and was far less grand than those closer to the main town. I parked my scooter by its entrance, which was a simple triangle formed by two large beams of wood. It was something to walk under, signifying that you were entering holy ground. The complex was small and simple, it was quiet, with very little signs of life. It was hot and dusty, the July sun baked everything.

The room with the Buddhas was easily missed, it lay off to the side by some bushes that looked desperate for water. I crouched as I stepped through the door. I closed my eyes and inhaled. The air was delectably damp from the lack of sun. There was so rarely any escape from the heat, but this long-standing structure felt like a cool basement.

The dozens of statues were almost all chipped, the pretty gold paint cracked and gathered on the dirt floor like sparkles to be swept up after a party. They seemed too old to touch, the air gradually turning the Buddha's eyes to sand. There was room for only one or two people. I sat down on a dilapidated rug and dug my toes into the dirt floor. I wanted to feel a kind of quiet in the marrow of my bones.

I began to wonder about belief. I wondered how you knew the difference between wanting to believe and believing. Were life's most challenging moments just obstacles placed before us, or was there some unexplained order or reason why people ended up on one particular path?

As I sat there, I questioned my own beliefs. I believe in the power of the universe, in energy, in a higher power. I use the word God, as what is within me and around me. I sometimes pray. Yet, I struggled to believe what my mother always tells me: that things will work out in the end. I wasn't sure that they would, and that frightened me. As I sat there among the Buddhas, I knew faith was still far away. In its place was fear that something would go wrong, that the thin rug I was now standing on would again be pulled out from beneath me, that Sam would not be coming home.

I thought about the great spiritual leaders, Gandhi or the Dalai Lama, and wondered if they ever felt doubt. I had met the Dalai Lama once in Montreal, as part of a group of reporters who sat in on a short talk before he addressed tens of thousands at our convention centre. There was a depth about His Holiness, an inspiring sense of calm, one that emanated outward. He was so awake, so powerfully in the present moment, that he almost radiated. As he made his way out of the room, he touched a few people and offered his thanks. I was already a bit starstruck to be standing next to another of the speakers that day, Deepak Chopra, but when the Dalai Lama stopped in front of me, the air that moved with him seemed to stop as well. He reached out and took my hands in his. His fingers were smooth and dry, and held mine gently. My entire being stood at attention, my eyes glued to his, unable to blink or look away. He paused, and as a playful grin stretched across his face, it felt as though I had, in some way, been chosen. Or blessed. There was such stillness in his grasp that he made me still. All he said was, "Be well."

Staring into the faces of the Buddhas in Thailand, I marvelled at how a human can generate the same quality of stillness as the stone these carvings were made from. I could have stayed in that holy place for hours, laid down and slept beside those statues, shared in their dreams, hoping to wake up feeling whole and full of answers. But outside I heard feet shuffling, pebbles scratching, and sandals slipping off. I took in every last expression, inhaled the sweet air, pulling the serenity deep into my lungs so I could hold it there. So I could hold onto it.

As I walked away, the worries I carried seemed less oppressive. Perhaps the Buddhas had held on to my doubt, unravelling it from me like a spool of thread, and buried it somewhere safe and sacred. Maybe they kept it because I didn't need it anymore. Maybe I was learning that faith didn't need to be explained or placed in a box or labelled something neat and tidy. Faith, I was learning, simply needed to be felt.

30 Trusting the Path

I often drove my scooter through the back roads of the island. The wind helped cool me down, I stumbled onto hidden beaches, stopped to buy young coconuts on the side of the road, stocked up on juicy mangoes, or ate yet another pad thai in my search for the tastiest. I liked to stare out at green hills and listen to the sound of bells ringing in the distance. I stopped to play with irresistible litters of puppies and kittens. I would find them living in boxes under tables on wat grounds, or in the backs of shops selling tank tops and shorts. They were so new to the world, snuggling close to their mothers.

Just beyond the garden of my bungalow was the town's main road from which two dogs, thin and silver-coated, would come to greet me each night. They had made their home not far from where I slept, and when they heard me coming, they yelped and nipped at each other, excited to have a meal they didn't have to dig up in a garbage dump. I poured out two generous piles of food for them then sat down under the stars and watched them gobble it down. Afterwards, they lay down at my feet, cuddled together, and we watched the island life unfold. After a quick scratch behind itchy ears, I bid them both good night. Off they ran, awake to the night's adventures.

A satisfying routine had set in: yoga classes, days by the water, chats with Satyia. It made me realize how quickly we can melt into a space and find a way to call it home. It's easy to create new habits—easier than we think. Time rubs away the edges of change, making it more palatable. But a new life, one I had worked long and hard to have, was within my grasp, and after twenty-eight days by the ocean, I packed my bags.

The afternoon of my departure, I found Satyia sitting on the balcony outside of my bungalow. Her legs were dangling off the edge, swinging like a child's, and she was fidgeting with a bracelet, moving each bead as if saying a prayer on a rosary. I sat down beside her. For several moments neither of us said a word. Satyia had no email or access to a telephone and, even if she did, she wouldn't have asked for either. Our lives had connected so briefly, and it was unlikely our paths would cross again. She wasn't mourning my departure as much as what my leaving meant for her. She would work and grow old here, her fate tied to this land.

"You will think of me Ta-rah?" Satyia still hadn't lifted her head to look at me, but that was what she asked. That was what she wanted. To be remembered. To know that someone out in a world she couldn't possibly imagine would know that she existed.

"I will think of you, I promise. I couldn't possibly forget you."

Pulling herself off the rail, she held out her arms and we hugged. Just for a moment she lay her head on my shoulder, but neither of us said goodbye: they were words we chose not to say.

"You go get your baby now?" she asked me.

"Yes. It's taken me a long time, but yes," I answered.

She hesitated for a moment, then smiled. "He a lucky baby Ta-rah."

I smiled back, moved by what it had taken for her to open up in that way.

"Thank you Satyia," I said. "That means a lot."

I watched her walk away, pushing her cleaning cart to the next room, her steps slow but steady. She didn't glance back.

A final wave was an offering she did not need or want. Satyia had no choice but to keep moving forward.

Thailand and its welcoming people had been a haven, a safe place to feel my feet, to walk slowly. To wait under the sitting tree for what life would drop from its precious leaves into my lap. But even in the most rapturous dwelling there is a time to rise up, to stare into the distance. Even if we can't see what's there, we have to go on faith that it is where we belong next. I didn't know what would happen, but I did know it included Sam. And that was all I needed to say a grateful and silent goodbye. With my joy, hope, anticipation and apprehension, along with whatever doubt still fastened itself to me packed carefully away, I boarded a plane back to Seoul.

Family

31 I Want It in My Bones

The guest house in Seoul was a functioning doll house, a shoe box, the secret room under the stairs where Harry Potter slept. There was space big enough for a single bed, a dresser, and a bathroom. A painting of a meadow hung above a bed in washed-out watercolours. The walls were white. There was no window. There was a phone, but no television. It was as different from the wide-open green spaces of Thailand as it could possibly be.

Like all major cities, Seoul is expensive. These rooms, run by the South Korean adoption agency, were a way to help ease the financial burden. Having no idea how long I was going to stay, I was grateful for my small room. Once my luggage was dropped off, my next stop was the adoption agency. What had a month brought? I was hoping for good news, the go-ahead to book our flights home. *Please*, I thought. *Please*.

"Hello Tarah, we have been expecting you," said Hyeyoung at the door.

It was so good to see her friendly face. She knew our story, she knew our baby, and that connection was something I badly needed. She helped me feel less alone.

"How was your last month?" she asked me.

"It was really wonderful. I'm happy to be back, though. I missed Sam."

"I'm sure you did," she said, lowering her eyes to the floor.

"Is there something wrong?" I asked her.

"No, nothing's wrong," she said. "It's just... the documents. They haven't arrived yet. We expected they would be here when you came back, but so far they have not come."

Just once, one damn time, I wanted something to be easy. "What does that mean?"

"I'm sure everything is fine," she said lightly. "Things just take longer sometimes. Don't worry."

"I'll try," I said, trying to appear understanding, when I didn't feel that way at all. "Tell me what we need exactly."

Hyeyoung explained that the court documents pronouncing us Sam's legal parents had yet to be translated into English, and, more importantly, the visa granting him permanent residency in Canada had not been delivered. The slow-moving wheels of adoption are the reason most parents choose to go back to their home country until all the necessary paperwork comes through. I had made a promise, though, to myself and my son: I would not leave Asia until we could leave together.

"The documents aren't ready," I told Enrico a few moments later. I'm the upbeat, positive one in our relationship. I knew I had to be that now, for him, even though I was feeling more like: *Please God, don't let something go wrong. Not now. Not again.* "They're sure it's just a question of a few more days," I added.

"What does that mean?" he asked. "How many days?"

"No one seems to know. I'm here, so we'll get daily updates. I'm sure we'll get news very soon."

"So, what do we do?" he asked, frustrated. "You've been gone so long already."

"I know. I feel it too."

"I miss you. I want you both home," he said.

"I miss you too. We will be. Soon."

Hyeyoung came to stand by my side after I had hung up with Enrico.

"All the news is not bad," she said with her shy grin.

"That's good," I laughed. "Some good news would be welcome."

Then came her question, the one that would change everything. "Would you like to take custody of your baby?"

"Yes! Yes, I would!" I wanted it in my bones.

Even though the court documents had yet to be translated, the Korean version pronouncing us Sam's legal guardians were ready. This was enough to allow me to take custody. I could not take him out of the country, but he could come and live with me. The waiting would continue, but we would do it together.

It wasn't everything I wanted after that long month away, but it was something. Hyeyoung laughed at my excitement, placing her hands in front of her mouth.

"We will begin your custody in stages," she said. "You will see him twice this week, and if the documents still don't arrive, you can take him with you next week. If they do arrive, you can take him home."

"I need to find somewhere bigger to live," I said. "And fast."

"Don't worry Tarah. We kept you the family room. You will have a kitchen and a window. It's a pretty room. You will move in one week."

"Thank you Hyeyoung," I said. "You have made everything easier. It means more than I can say."

"You will see," she said, bowing her head. "Everything will be fine."

Waiting for that first hour for Sam was like waiting for summer—it felt eternal. When he arrived, he seemed taller already. It had only been a month, but when I sat with him in the playroom, I was sure he had grown. I knew he didn't recognize me; that part was crushing. I wanted to pull him into my arms, cover him with kisses, whisper how much I had missed him. In the life of someone only fifteen months old, though, twenty-eight days is forever. I had to move at his pace. We had only met twice, but I had memorized so much. I knew the exact colour of his eyes, the way his hair fell into his face, the two round beauty marks that graced his left wrist.

I wondered again what I had missed, what new and wonderful moments he had experienced without us. I asked his foster mother Soo about his care: what he ate, when he slept, what toys he liked best, what made him laugh or cry.

"You will be a good mother Tarah," said Hyeyoung encouragingly. "You will know what to do."

"I just want to make sure I ask everything now," I explained. "I will be alone with him in just a few days. I'm excited and terrified at the same time."

"I will be here if you need me, but you won't need me. I'm sure," said Hyeyoung. "But now we must go."

Again, the hour passed all too quickly. I touched his face and once again he looked me straight in the eyes. I was spellbound. I kissed him, his skin creamy as butterscotch. On the walk back to my bland room, I felt melancholic. The days ahead, the hours until our next visit, were going to be long and lonely.

32 The Horrifying Story of Comfort Women

It was oppressively humid, the air syrupy, like walking through a swamp. I wandered around Seoul feeling homesick. The thirteen-hour time difference meant my days were still Enrico's nights, and time fought me at every turn. Reading, sleeping, walking, writing: no matter how I tried to fill the days, there was a weight to them as oppressive and disagreeable as the weather.

There was a beautiful wat a twenty-minute walk from my room. Once inside the grounds, hundreds of white lanterns hung low from the ceiling, creating a cloud-like canopy that offered shelter from the world outside. Candles in shimmery orange holders lined a pebbled walkway that led to an open space where a giant Buddha towered over trees and rooftops. I pulled over a cushion and sat down hoping to find a sense of calm. It would not come. *Breathe. Breathe.* Nope. There was no stillness inside me. My mind was full of questions, anxiety simmered. After a month in Thailand, I felt like a failure. *So much for that,* I thought. I thanked the Buddha, anticipating that he would understand. *I need to move.* So I left and walked through parks and into shopping malls, down sidewalks by six-lane highways, across busy clothing and technology districts, through back alleys, food markets, and around tourist sites.

I walked and walked, always ending up back at my windowless room.

At the end of each day, the relief from the heat was delicious. I sat on the stone steps outside the guest house with a bottle of cold Korean beer, watching the city's lights turn on one coloured bulb at a time. Restaurants grew busy, cars honked to secure coveted parking spots. Pretty people spilled out into the streets. The night awoke a new kind of energy in Seoul, bolder and braver, one filled with hand-holding and stolen kisses.

The guest house had an old doorman who spent his afternoons in a dimly lit lobby behind a beaten-down desk. At night he almost always joined me on the steps. He shuffled out, the black soles of his sandals scraping across the tiles. His name was Sun, and he was in his seventies, with a full head of thick, white hair, and crevices of wrinkles on his face. He lowered himself, settling onto the hard surface as if into a favourite chair. More than once he pulled out a piece of dried fish or Korean pancake from a brown paper bag to share with me. He grinned as I tasted it, happy to offer an edible gesture of friendship.

We talked most evenings. He spoke not a word of English, and I knew only a few words in Korean, but it didn't seem to matter. I think we both wanted the company. I told him about Sam, or about my day, and what he shared I had no idea but his tender voice filled an ever-growing space inside of me that craved closeness.

Some nights we simply sat together in silence watching the vibrant blues of the sky grow opaque. When our bodies ached too much, our bones too stiff from leaning into the stone steps, I bid Sun goodnight and walked the five flights of stairs to my room.

I always paused on the third floor, which had been a mystery to me since my return to Seoul. There was no long corridor with doors on either side like every other floor, just one large set of double doors that led somewhere unknown. I had never seen those doors open, nor what was behind them, but there were always muffled sounds and a sense of movement. Women, dressed in pale pastels, came and went from the building at all hours, shuffling up and down the stairs to the third floor. What they did behind those double doors was like a whisper uttered too softly to understand.

One hazy morning, five long days before Sam was to come into my life for good, I sat flipping through a Korean tourist guide. How would I spend another day without my child? A paragraph about a museum caught my attention. It was in a part of the city I had yet to explore. Finding it would be my activity for the day, filling the hours that stretched before me like lanes of highway.

After a long subway ride and a ten-minute walk down a busy four-lane street, I spotted a faded, yellow arrow pointing left. Under the arrow was written, simply, "Museum". It pointed toward a narrow alleyway, not even a street, past residential buildings, empty parking garages, and an active construction site. When I finally saw the entrance, it was a grey, metal door on the side of a sparse hill. "The War and Women's Human Rights Museum" was carved into the steel.

The museum was made up of a few rooms spread over two modest floors. The exhibit guided you through the horrifying circumstances experienced by comfort women. This is yet another horrific part of human history. As far back as the First World War and through the Second World War, thousands upon thousands of women from several countries including China, Korea, and Indonesia were kidnapped and imprisoned in so-called comfort centres. Torn from their families when they were as young as thirteen years old, these women were kept as sex slaves for Japanese military men. The women endured endless acts of rape and abuse over many years.

Old newspaper clippings, yellowed and torn at the edges, covered the museum walls. They were pictures, notes, advertisements, messages, all disconsolate pleas from families searching for daughters gone missing, snatched away so suddenly that only ghosts were left behind to mourn or bury. Those who did make it home were no longer girls with eyes wide open to the world, but women beaten down from years of cruel and ceaseless violations.

Wide panels hung on ochre walls, explaining how comfort centres were initiated and sustained by the Japanese government during its occupation of Korea. As the Japanese territory increased in size, the number of centres grew as well, and hundreds appeared along the Pacific Rim. When the first shocking stories of what comfort women had endured began to surface in the early 1990s, it was as if a dam had breached, and story after story gushed out. The museum contained numerous videos, playing over and over again as if caught in a time loop, of now-elderly women recounting their years of torture. Often, they were sobbing. The women spoke in Korean, so I could not understand their words, but the essence of what they shared was clear.

I learned about how women have been gathering and protesting outside of the Japanese Embassy in Seoul every Wednesday since 1992. They are demanding that the Japanese government apologize to the women for creating these camps, for what they and their families had been forced to endure, and to offer some kind of accountability. I watched videos of the protests, by women, their daughters, and their daughters' daughters, all demanding to be heard.

I left the museum feeling sombre, shocked at what humans are capable of doing to each other and what some are capable of surviving. But do you really survive? Many of the women in the videos had died, and those who lived continued to fight for recognition, telling and retelling their stories until they are heard.

33 In Like a Lion Came Motherhood

The night before I took custody of Sam, Enrico and I spent longer than usual on our daily video chat. I whispered to him in the dark while the sun rose on his side of the world.

"Tomorrow he'll be ours," I said.

"You'll be wonderful. You have been waiting for this moment for so long."

"I wish you were here," I said.

"Me too. More than anything. But I know you'll be exactly who he needs."

"I'll be in touch as soon as I can."

"I'll be waiting."

We let the silence live between us. It took a long time before I finally fell asleep.

"Are you ready?" Hyeyoung asked the next morning.

"I am. I've been ready for years," I said.

"I know you are," she said. "Let's go in then. This is a big day."

We pushed open the doors to the adoption agency and greeted Sam's foster family. I had seen Soo, his foster mother, twice since I had returned to Seoul. She was wearing a long, sky-blue dress with big, pink flowers, and the necklace Enrico and I had given her as a gift, a silver chain with a carved rose in its centre. She had dressed up for the occasion with grey eyeshadow swept across her lids and burgundy gloss on her lips. Beside Soo, was her husband, whom I had not met. He was tall, with a warm face that pulled down into a square jaw, and when he took my hand in his, he squeezed gently. It was going to be an agonizing morning for us all.

This couple had been Sam's family, his lifeline, and today they were saying goodbye. The only woman Sam had ever known as mother was struggling through her final moments with him. Her husband held her forearm gently in his palm, as if that action could help hold her up.

She didn't kiss Sam goodbye. Instead, she took a lingering look at his face, as if committing as much as she could to memory. Scooping his hands into hers, she held them to her cheek for one short moment, then closed her eyes. When she opened them, it was over. She had made whatever farewell she had to make.

She turned to me and said something in Korean. Hyeyoung swallowed slowly and said, "She asks you to give him a good life."

I bowed my head, and she did the same. We stayed like that for several minutes, trying to catch our breath, making a small human connection in a big world where two women from very different lives cherished one little boy.

"I will," I promised. "I will give him a good life."

With adoption, there is no pregnancy to prepare you for parenthood. No birth that gives way to the moment your child is first placed in your arms. For adoptive parents, it happens in one indescribable moment when a child's hand is placed in yours, and, just like that, you are a mother or a father. Yet to him I was a stranger. Even though I had met Sam, he did not know me, and his confusion was palpable. He stayed close to Hyeyoung as we walked away from his foster family, turning back several times as if wondering why they were not following.

Hyeyoung walked us back to our guest house, made sure we had milk, diapers, and food. She then closed the door behind her. She knew what she was leaving us to face. She had seen it before.

When the door shut and the lock clicked into place, Sam was like an animal caught in a trap. He looked around frantically for an exit, and when he realized there was none, he began sobbing uncontrollably.

He did not stop for two full days.

I held my weeping baby in my arms for hours on end as he mourned what had been precious to him: his life, his family. He was suffering a tear in the fabric of everything he knew. It was heartbreaking to watch one so young grieve with such overwhelming emotion. I had been told to expect this reaction, but no amount of knowledge could have prepared me for the depth of his distress. He ran to the door of our room, banged on it with his fists, desperate to escape back to the world that he knew. When that didn't work, he banged on the door with his head. It was almost as if he understood the rupture was permanent, and was utterly unable to cope with all the suffering it brought.

It broke my heart. Down on my knees, I crawled as close to him as he allowed, desperate to help in any way I could. I would have done anything to take away his heartache, to make his burden mine. But it was his to carry, even at his tender age. With tears pouring down his face, two streams of rushing water, he fought it for as long as he could before throwing himself into my arms. I held him to me tightly while he just cried and cried. We did nothing else—we neither ate nor slept. It was only when the sun went down, that he collapsed into sleep. When he woke, though, and came face to face again with his new reality, fear attacked quickly, violently, and he broke down once again into relentless weeping.

We were both exhausted, but I had never felt so inexplicably powerful in my life. My entire being felt devoted to this one task of caring for him. I was awake in my very core. This child, only fifteen months old, felt alone in the world, and I was the only person he had to help him find his way. It took endless hours of compassion to soothe him. It was the start of our relationship, and tough as that beginning was, we were creating a bond of tenderness and trust. I held him, fed him, bathed him, and wiped him down with a soft cloth. I comforted him and worked on making him feel safe again. I slept by his side. I sang to him. I loved him.

I spoke to Enrico in the moments when Sam slept, to hear his voice, to share precious moments, to comfort my husband and to feel comforted by him. I spoke to no one else. For five long days, the door to our guesthouse did not open once. It's called cocooning: keeping your newly adopted baby away from other people and the outside world to encourage attachment at every level. To make sure that child will come to you when he needs comfort, food, or care. Those who care for us when we feel alone become our lifelines, and this is what needs to be cultivated in a new baby, in order to create a bond first of need, then of love.

Sam and I stayed there together, the days melting into nights, the world outside inaccessible to us both. We clung to each other, growing together like vines in search of sun. Watching him struggle and bearing witness to the strength he found to live through his anguish was the most extraordinary experience of my life.

Slowly, came sweet smiles, gentle cuddling and nights spent curled together. Sam's memories were fading, settling into a place where they didn't frighten him. It was just the two of us, and we needed each other. Life changed profoundly for us both. Sam began holding onto me, touching my cheeks, exploring my face with his eyes. He held my hand as he fell asleep, making sure I would be there when he woke. I never left his side. We had made it through the dark, out of that dreadful place. Through indescribable sorrow, Sam found what he needed to move on: love.

34 The Strike

"Tell me more about him," Enrico said.

"He's sweet, loving, funny. And he has the most incredible smile I've ever seen. He climbs on everything. He won't stop opening the fridge. He sleeps with his bum in the air, which is beyond adorable."

Enrico was laughing. "You sound so happy."

"I am. We are. Now we just need to come home."

"How do you spend your days?" he asked.

"We still haven't left the guest house. We're getting to know each other, thankfully the most difficult period is behind us. It's heaven, really."

"I wish I could have been there, for you both," he said. "I wish I could be there."

"I know that. Our life together will begin soon. I promise."

"Is he asleep?" he asked.

"He is. It's so hot right now that we nap as often as possible. Now, tell me, what do you know about the strike."

Unbelievably, we were facing yet another unforeseen obstacle.

"It's not good," he said. "Nobody knows how bad it will get, or what it will mean for children being adopted. But it's not good."

Canada's foreign embassy workers were on strike. The employees who processed visas had walked off the job. The strike, over wages, affected anyone requiring a Canadian visa, including students, temporary workers, and tourists. The visas required for adopted children to enter Canada were also processed in those centres, the stacks of files no doubt growing taller by the day.

News reports estimated the strike would delay visas by weeks, if not months. It affected about 150 workers in fifteen of the largest immigration processing centres in the world, including New Delhi, London, and Beijing. The staff were also on strike in Manila where Sam's visa was now stuck in the cog of a giant machine that had ground to a halt.

"There has to be something we can do," I said.

"I'm getting as much information as I can," Enrico answered. "We'll figure this out."

I could tell he felt as unsure as I did.

You have got to be kidding me, was how I was feeling. *No fucking way,* was another. Pulling Sam into my arms, I said a silent thank you that I had stayed in Asia. If I had left with Enrico, I would have been separated from my child by oceans and continents. Whatever was going to happen, however long it was going to take to get home, at least we were together. And that made everything else easier to bear.

"Are adopted children a priority?" I asked.

"I haven't gotten a straight answer on that," said Enrico. "But how could they not be?"

Some files were still processed on humanitarian grounds, but we didn't know if that included adopted children. Enrico took on the task with the ferocity of a new father. He contacted government officials at all levels pushing everyone to add their voice to those trying to get these children home.

Hyeyoung arrived at my door a few nights later. It had been a week since I had taken custody of Sam. She brought someone new with her.

"This is Kyunghwa," she explained. "She is the manager of Korea's Adoption Agency. She would like to ask you a favour."

"Hello," I said. "How can I help you?"

"We need you to help us write a letter," she said.

Kyunghwa had been fielding calls from parents in the final stages of adoption. Parents for whom news of the strike shattered a fragile hold that was keeping desperation from pushing to the surface. She had no answers, had received no visas, and could offer no reassuring words. We were all at the mercy of a government wage war, hoping the battle would be over soon.

"Can you help?" asked Kyunghwa.

"Of course," I said. "Tell me what you want to say."

We crafted a strongly worded letter to Canadian embassy officials in Manila explaining that adopted children needed to be paired with their new parents as quickly as possible. Any delay could have an impact on the child's attachment and development with a new family. And that could influence an entire life.

"Do you think it will help?" I asked her.

"I do, it must." said Kyunghwa, and she thanked me.

"You are welcome. Don't hesitate to let me know if you need anything else."

"You are by yourself here," she said. "You will be OK?"

"I will be OK," I said. "I have my baby."

I was the only adoptive parent currently in Seoul. The only one who had taken custody of her child. I emailed the two other Quebec families I had met in Seoul, telling them I was back, with Sam, and that they too could return and take custody. Our friendships bloomed quickly. I was on the ground in Seoul as they navigated how soon to return when so much was uncertain. We shared our fears and our hopes. I grew ever closer to Muriel in particular, whose baby was born five weeks before Sam. We exchanged emails often, offering what comfort we could. Her child remained with his foster family, while I could hold my baby at night. We all waited while officials negotiated and workers made demands. All we could do was wait. And I had become good at that.

35 Divine Destiny

While a lengthy period of cocooning is highly encouraged, after a week in our room, where our bond had taken a gentle but firm hold, both Sam and I were going stir-crazy. We opened the door and spent the morning exploring the hallway outside our room. This included the area where the sheets and towels for the five floors of the guest house were washed. Large, white machines beckoned with knobs and buttons for pushing and pulling, and clear glass windows where soapy water swirled linens around and around like ghosts playing a game of catch-me-if-you-can.

A separate room housed a fridge and an oversized sink with shiny metal faucets. Sam examined every nook and cranny, pushed every button, touched every clasp, latch, and lever with the determination of an explorer. His inspection complete, we walked to the end of our long corridor and stared out the one window. His arm was wrapped around my neck as we peered onto the streets beyond, marvelling at pink-tiled roofs and trees draped in bright yellow flowers. We watched cars go by and listened to horns honking in the distance.

He had still not spoken since we had come together as mother and son. I don't know if he babbled or made baby noises while he lived with Soo. But with me, he was silent. Even if he had said something, we had no shared language. The way he communicated was with his eyes.

He glanced from the window to me and eventually laid his head against mine. I kissed him on the forehead and then on each cheek, letting him know the only way I could that I would never, ever leave him.

The hallway with its shadows and pale grey walls wasn't much, but it expanded the world we had been sharing. On the ninth day we took the elevator down into the lobby, and Sam met Sun, the doorman who had so often kept me company in the evening. Sun was so excited to meet my little boy that he shined. He let Sam play with his telephone, and when Sam lost interest in that, he gave him pieces of paper to fold and keep in the pocket of his shorts like buried treasure. Sun spoke to my child in Korean, and I saw him nod.

I knew it was important that I speak to Sam. What I said didn't matter all that much. It was the tone, the communication, the validation of his every emotion that was meaningful. I talked about his father, about a whole new family in Canada that was eager to meet him. I told him bedtime stories and, when I saw sadness creep onto his face, I explained that we were together, he would never be alone, that he would always, always be my darling boy. I told him often that he was my baby, forever and ever and ever.

Another week passed with still no news from the embassy, no answer as to when we could go home. Employees were still on strike but some visas— those granted on humanitarian grounds—were being issued. We still had no idea if adopted children were among that group.

"There's still no news on this end," Enrico said angrily. "It's infuriating."

"We haven't heard anything here either," I told him.

"How are you both doing?"

"We're good," I said. "I'll send you more pictures."

"I look forward to every one," he answered. "It makes me miss you more, though. I'm worried how much longer this is going to take."

"I feel the same way. But we have come so far, unimaginably far. It's the home stretch."

The days passed. The simmering Korean summer kept us locked inside most afternoons. The early mornings, though, were cool and fresh. Before the suffocating heat of the day settled in, Sam and I went exploring for parks and food. With his body nestled close to mine in the baby carrier, we bought plump asian pears and sweet mandarins, blocks of tofu, eggs and tea that tasted like brown rice, honey and ginger. We wandered into outdoor markets where the air was thick with the smell of vinegar and cooked fish. I bought rolls of gimbap, rice and marinated vegetables rolled in deep green sheets of seaweed. We ate with our hands, and moist rice stuck to our lips. We beamed at each other while sharing a frozen desert, and I watched him licking sticky, sweetness from his spoon.

People stared at us. A Korean baby and a white woman with long, red hair were an unusual sight in our un-touristy neighbourhood. I couldn't tell if it was judgement or simple curiosity, likely a bit of both. Although foreign adoption was frowned upon by some locals, I was so happy and grateful that I was immune from negativity. When I did catch the eyes of those staring, mostly women, I smiled, and they usually smiled back.

On late-afternoon walks Sam fell asleep, drifting off to the rhythm of my steps, and I found a shaded bench in a park where I would think back to the sitting tree, and would listen to him breathe. It was like listening to the wingbeats of a butterfly. Stroking his fine baby hair, I held him as tightly as I could without waking him up. Staring at his perfect features, his flawless sleeping face. I ached with a love I had not known existed.

Most days, we made our way to the adoption agency, which was just a few doors down from the guest house. We stepped off the elevator and through a hallway peppered with strollers, boxes of diapers and toys, and opened the door. "It's Sam! Here comes Sam!"

The entire office came to know us. Seeing them became an important part of our day.

"We're happy to see you," said Hyeyoung.

I knew just by looking at her, there had been no news. "Nothing?" I asked anyway.

She shook her head.

Sam took over the playroom where we had spent a few early hours together, in what felt like another life, when he was not yet my son and I not yet his mother. Hyeyoung and Kyunghwa were the only two people I knew who spoke English. Sensing my loneliness and a longing for home, they were endlessly accommodating.

"Tell me about your day with Sam," Kyunghwa asked.

We talked, sitting together on the office couch, sipping savoury tea. Kyunghwa had fascinating eyes: one brown and one sky-blue. A milky blue, as if clouds had been mixed in and swirled about.

"I can see he's more comfortable every day," she said.

"My boys were like animals this morning!" laughed Hyeyoung. As always when she broke into a grin, her delicate hands shot up to cover her mouth. "I didn't think I would get them to school," she joked. "But Sam, he will be good, I'm sure."

We all turned to gaze at him as he determinedly pulled a red truck across a blue mat. He must have sensed us, because he stopped what he was doing. He watched us watching him for just a moment, then went back to his task. I knew that Hyeyoung and Kyunghwa had to be busy, but they always put work aside when I arrived. They never made me feel I was disturbing them.

"Come, Tarah," they said. "The babies are arriving!"

On certain days the adoption offices became a flurry of activity as foster mothers and babies dropped by for check-ups, weighings, and tests. This brought a wonderful energy to our otherwise quiet life. I wondered where all those babies would end up. Sam had been one of them, selected for a foster family, evaluated, then somehow chosen for us. It seemed impossible that any other baby could have been ours, yet the randomness felt unsettling. Was it just luck or timing that brought Sam and me together? Could it be that simple? Or was it something grander, like destiny—divine, beautiful, destiny—that he was meant for us all along? I felt, profoundly, that it was destiny.

When the adoption department, and to some degree, our neighbourhood, shut down on weekends, Sam and I wandered around, listened to church bells, and watched families play badminton in the park. Weekends moved at a sluggish pace and in hushed tones. With Sun not at his post, even the guest house had a quiet, haunted feeling.

As impatient as I felt, I knew our unusual circumstance was giving us what most adopted families do not have: time. Time together in the child's own country. Time alone where the smells, people and sounds were still familiar to him. It was a cushion to soften the edge of so much change.

Already Sam came to me for food and to play and, more importantly, when he needed to be held, when he wanted protection, when he had to be soothed. During meals, he offered me pieces of whatever was on his plate, determinedly placing them in my hand and then staring intently until I popped something into my mouth. I saw his sharing as a sign of acceptance. He held me close as he fell asleep, and in the morning he wakened me by leaning his head against mine like a cat. My life with Sam took on a kind of surreal beauty. He needed me. And I believed he was coming to care for me.

As the days passed, though, I was increasingly impatient to get home. Hyeyoung and Kyunghwa understood the weight of my waiting, but they could offer me no salve. When I asked about Sam's visa, they exchanged a glance and always said the same thing.

"Sorry Tarah, no news. Maybe tomorrow."

36 He Can't Leave So I Can't Leave

Sharp rays of orange pierced through our window. There was an unexpected knock at our door, and when I opened it, Hyeyoung and Kyunghwa were there with an older woman I did not recognize. They slid off their shoes, came inside, and sat down in the living area. The older woman, they told me, was the director of the Korean Adoption Agency— Hyeyoung and Kyunghwa's immediate superior.

"How are you today?" they asked. They were unusually silent, and it was clear the tidings they brought were not good.

"I'm well," I said. "Do you want to tell me what's wrong?"

All three women kept their hands wound firmly in their laps.

"It is not easy to explain," began Kyunghwa. "There has been a development."

And just like that the air around us grew eerily still. They spoke in Korean amongst themselves for a few moments, then Kyunghwa began.

"We received the visas, Tarah," she said. "But not all of them."

Her eyes remained fixed to mine, and I knew whatever she had come to say, it would not be easy. I remained silent until Kyunghwa spoke again.

"We received visas for the other two Canadian families," she continued, "but Tarah, we did not receive one for Sam."

"Sam didn't get a visa?" I asked. "Why?"

"We do not know."

"What does that mean? How can he not have a visa? What could that possibly mean?"

"We do not know," she said again. "I'm sorry."

No. No. No. No. No.

Tears dripped down my face, silent tears, the kind that come to take the place of words. Sam stopped playing and ran over to me, his feet slapping the bare floor. He crawled into my lap as if it were a haven, tucked his head under my neck and wrapped his arms around my chest. My baby, fresh from his own hurt, was not able to handle mine. He was too fragile. I stroked his head, whispering to him that everything was going to be alright.

"Tell me what you know," I whispered.

"We received the other visas," Kyunghwa explained, "but the embassy in Manila does not seem to recognize Sam's file or his status. They didn't offer any explanation," she continued. "The embassy would only say..." Kyunghwa's voice trailed off. Her one blue and one brown eye were unable to look at me.

"What?" I asked her. "What did they say?"

"They said," she began again, "that they would not be issuing him a visa."

"How is that possible?"

This. Can. Not. Be. Happening.

My mind began running down some very frightening roads, searching for an escape, longing for one safe path that would lead us home.

"We are not sure yet," she said, "but we will find out."

"What if we just left?" I asked urgently. "What if we got on a plane and dealt with everything once we landed in Canada? I know it's not ideal, but at least we would be home."

The three women spoke quietly in Korean, their heads bent close together as if they were sharing a secret.

"They will not let you leave, Tarah," Kyunghwa said at last. "Or more clearly, they will not let Sam leave. I know it's difficult," she said, "but that is just not an option."

It was hard to speak. Or to breathe.

"What do we do now?" I asked, as scared and helpless as I had ever been in my life.

"I'm not sure," Kyunghwa said honestly. "But we will figure something out. I promise. Sleep now."

And just like that, they left.

Dread began to take hold. It burned feverish and red in my belly. What if they took Sam from me? What if there was nothing I could do to stop it from happening? The pressure behind my eyes began to sting. I sat there, still as a bird on a branch, holding my baby and praying that life would not fail us. That what had brought us together and the love that had already taken root in us both would not be pulled apart, too young and fragile to survive the tear. I did not think I could bear it. I would wither and die without him. Our lives had been intertwined, binding us together so that one could not live without the other. I kissed Sam's head, and begged whatever God was listening to help us.

Please God. Please. Please.

"How can this be happening?" Enrico demanded. "And what does it mean?"

"It means we won't be coming back just yet," I said, "but we'll figure this out."

It had been one month since I had landed back in Korea from Thailand.

"What does this mean?" he asked again.

"I don't know. I don't know."

The following morning Sam and I arrived at the adoption office where Kyunghwa and I crafted an urgent email to Canadian embassy officials in Manila. We asked for a Canadian residency visa for Sam, reminding them that he had been legally adopted in a Korean court by a Canadian family and needed immediate entry into Canada. We attached all relevant documents, certain they had every possible piece of information. All there was to do now was wait.

Again.

"I'm calling everyone I can think of," Enrico said. "Somebody, somewhere has to be able to help us. Or at least help us understand what's going on. It just doesn't make any sense."

"I'm scared," I confessed.

"I know," he said. "We'll figure this out. He's our baby. Remember that."

Night fell once more. Another day had passed. I didn't feel like talking, even to my husband, so, as his morning began and our night took hold, I placed the tablet where he could watch Sam as he slept, hear him breathe. He began singing a lullaby. Soon, I was asleep as well.

"They wrote back," Kyunghwa said into the phone the next morning. "You should come now."

"It's only been one day. Does that mean it's good news?" I asked.

"No Tarah, it's not."

I couldn't believe it when I read the email from the embassy. I had to read it over and over again even though it contained only a single sentence. It read: We do not recognize the child in question. We will not be issuing a visa.

That was it. No explanation. No answers. No help.

"Can they take him from me?" I asked Kyunghwa. "What if we can't figure this out? Can I lose him?"

"No, Tarah," she said, as firmly as she had ever spoken. "He is your son, and I promise you nothing can change that. We will find an answer."

I had to believe her. I knew, however, that until I was on a plane out of the country, anxiety and doubt would creep around inside me like a hungry animal searching for food. Enrico and I discussed his coming back to South Korea, but ultimately it seemed wiser to have someone in Canada who could make calls and badger officials until someone could tell us what needed to happen next. My husband spent the following week at a command centre created on our dining room table, contacting government officials. The problem was that we didn't know why Sam was being refused a visa. How can you solve a problem when you don't know why it exists?

I finally had my baby. I just couldn't bring him home.

37 The Boy and the Rivière Noire

My dreams became restless.

I dreamt of loss and horror I had seen up close in a story that I had reported on and that I have never forgotten.

It was one week before Christmas. In a remote Quebec town blanketed by crystalline winter snow, the unimaginable happened. A six-year-old boy, whose family had long lived by the shores of the Rivière Noire, walked too closely to its banks and slipped inside. The freezing water must have claimed him quickly, and the fast-moving current swept him away. His older brother, frantic, ran for help, ran for his father, begging him to undo what life had snatched from his grasp. His father, a large man, ran to the river, the laces of his boots undone, his coat unzipped despite the cold, shouting, screaming, begging the river to return his son to him. He searched the ice, transparent in places, for a coat visible under the water, for anything that would lead him to his child. He did not find a single trace. He dropped to his knees, and with his face in his hands, sobbed.

Within minutes, calls for help rushed out over lines like racehorses and all available emergency personnel from nearby towns across eastern and southern Quebec arrived by the banks of the river. Firefighters used sharp metal picks to break through ice near the shore, police officers scoured the woods throwing aside thick brush weighed down by snow, divers in yellow plastic suits with ropes tied around their waists inched forward seeking a hand they could pull to the surface.

Within two hours, the media arrived, reporters and satellite trucks, camera crews and writers. I stared out into the Rivière Noire and asked it to be forgiving. The media represented the eyes and ears of a province of eight million people who seemed to collectively pray for the life of that boy.

Christmas was four days away.

The hours dragged on, the agonizing search clawed forward with nothing to show for all the time spent. Visibility shrank, and as the last tenuous rays of light faded, the search was called off. It was renamed, too. It was no longer a search and rescue, but a search and recovery. They were now looking for a body.

Reporters drove back to their stations. Stories got written, words were spoken, but there were no answers and there was no solace. We told people that today there was no happy ending. We explained that at dawn the search for this little boy, for his body, would begin again. We showed video of rescue divers and aired interviews of their greatest concern— that if he was not found soon, one freezing day would cause the sliced-up ice over the river to reform, and his small body would stay frozen there until spring. A sky-coloured tomb, under the ice.

That night, back from the banks of the river, dolour clung to me like soot, and there was no washing it away. It ate next to me, watched me bathe, curled by my side in my bed.

I lay awake that night and imagined the firefighters and rescue divers home with their families. They would have arrived too late to say goodnight, so they would have tip-toed into their children's bedrooms and stared at their sleeping faces and thought: there but for the grace of God. A tender kiss would be placed on the children's foreheads, and a wish of sweet dreams. Then they would sit wearily at their kitchen tables, their heads in their hands, a bowl of steaming soup set before them. "Eat," a lover or partner would say, placing a loving hand on a shoulder. "It will be a short night."

Unable to sleep, I wondered if that boy's mother had found even one hour free of nightmares. I imagined her eyes swollen, curled in the bed of her other son, refusing to leave, unable to let him go, her arms wrapped around his chest, her face buried in his hair. I imagined his father awake, standing and staring out toward the glutenous river, disbelief and anguish tearing at him, his very being shattered into too many pieces to ever pick up.

We were back the next morning, and the search for the boy's body had begun again. The police divers in their bright orange and yellow suits bobbed in the water. They looked bright as balloons, pulled down to the river's bottom, then released, shooting to the surface and breaking through with a great, shuddering gasp. Ice breakers moved meticulously, cutting through thick sheets. Low-flying helicopters scanned the surface while officers continued to break through the brush, just in case he had made it onto the shore.

The mother stayed away. The father walked by occasionally, his face grey as damp paper. He stopped to speak into our microphones.

"We must find him," he said. "It is the most important thing in the world to me right now."

He could no more leave the banks of the river than he could leave his child in its waters all winter long. It was too cold, and he was too young. This father could not save his son, there was nothing he could do to help search, so he braced himself.

"I want him with me," he said. "I need him with me."

On day two, divers found something: the family dog was frozen and trapped under the ice not far from where the boy had fallen in. Perhaps the dog had jumped into the water to rescue the child and the river took the pup as well. Family and friends, even strangers, arrived to keep vigil. So that the boy would not be alone. But they did not find him, not on that day.

Another brief night. Temperatures dropped. The search became more frantic. Emergency personnel were exhausted, pushing ahead with every last ounce of strength, nerves stretched and strained like a muscle right before a tear. We learned from an aunt that the boy would have turned seven on January fifth, weeks away from a birthday.

On the fourth day, they found him.

Police divers pulled his body from the river 400 metres from where he had fallen in. Wrapped in a plastic tarp, he was brought into a makeshift tent, a morgue, where his parents needed to enter and see for themselves—they needed to identify their child and witness the unspeakable. Firefighters broke down, mothers and grandmothers wrapped their pillowy arms around them, wiping away their devastation and offering thanks.

"Thank you for searching," they said.

"We are all fathers," they answered back.

When the boy's mother left the tent, her face was ghostly white. She had grief to tend to: it was demanding and it would not be ignored. The father followed, his boots still undone, the laces wet and muddy brown, his coat still unzipped.

"We are relieved," he told us, half-moon puddles under his eyes, "because he is with us now." His head dropped and his lips pulled together. "There is one more angel in heaven," he said. "My son is at peace."

He turned and walked away, perhaps toward his wife, where they would seek out some infinitesimal space in the world where their suffering was not so acute. Perhaps over time, they would chip away at that place, making it larger, so that they could walk freely without death at their heels.

Reporters returned to their stations, we filed our stories, answered the heart-wrenching question asked by the people—yes, yes, the child was found. He was no longer at the bottom of the river but lodged firmly and forever in the minds of those who treasured him. Christmas was twenty-four hours away.

That father is etched in my mind's eye, his strength, how he wore it on his shoulders with such grace, how he never seemed to waver under the massive, penetrating pressure of so much suffering. Invisible wounds take up so much space and take eons to heal. Millimetre by millimetre the delicate flesh pulls together. It takes love and patience. But above all it is time, the passing of days, the surrendering of the months, the letting go of the years. Time is the only way to get far enough from the wretchedness so that it doesn't ache as profoundly. Time can give you distance, and distance, eventually, can bring you peace.

38 Silver Linings

Days drifted into nights and another week passed. Sam and I found ease in our routine: walking, playing, eating, exploring. We video chatted with Enrico, my parents, and my sister. At night I read novels and watched world news on our small TV. And still we waited. There was always the waiting.

When dreams disturbed my sleep, Sam and I would curl up on our bed in the late morning, close the blinds, and then fall into a deeper sleep. We would wake in a sweat, our hair sticking to our foreheads like dew-drenched blades of grass. Then we would sit on the windowsill with cool water and watch the slow movement of people on the streets below.

His smile came easily now; even in those early weeks of uncertainty and change, there was joy. Whatever fear he had come with, my baby boy had found a place for it. Somewhere hidden where it would dissipate until eventually disappearing forever. Sorrow, too, had slipped away, taking with it the dark of his eyes, leaving in its place the rich brown of cocoa beans and mud pies.

With our every minute spent together, the bond between Sam and I had grown stronger and more solid. There was still work to be done, of course. Our foundation had only just been poured. It wasn't yet resilient enough to withstand harsh storms or shaky ground. Slowly, though, it was solidifying into something that would. What precious thing being built does not need time and patience?

Once a week, the Korean Social Welfare Society welcomed single mothers into the play area of the guest house where we lived. It was a way of helping these mothers by offering a space where they could come together without judgment.

One of the organizers knocked on our door, and invited us to join them. Games were organized, prizes, made up of body creams and boxes of tea, were given out, the children entertained and fed.

The mothers seemed happy to be among those who had chosen a similar path—keeping their children rather than giving them up for adoption. Sam and I were an example of what would have happened had they made a different choice. They stared at me with questions they could not ask and I could not answer. I felt awkward because I wasn't sure if they saw me as an enemy. I felt strangely guilty to be among them, as if I was taking something that didn't belong to me. My baby played with their babies and, as I sat there quietly, it seemed as if an unspoken understanding grew between us. They had made their choices, other women had made theirs, and I had made mine, and here we were, all of us mothers.

Walking back to our room, we passed the double doors of the third floor. As always, women came and went wearing flower-coloured hospital scrubs. An entire world seemed to ebb and flow in constant movement behind those doors. I knew by then there were babies inside—children given for adoption before being placed with a foster family—but I never once heard a baby cry.

The caretakers we saw on the steps or in the lobby occasionally offered a half-smile to Sam. They barely acknowledged me, though. They kept their eyes down and mostly pretended I wasn't there. Occasionally there was a quick nod of the head, like the snapping of a rubber band, but never any eye contact. I wasn't sure if I was unwelcome, or if their lack of warmth was protocol to Western parents. I knew my continued presence was unusual, for families usually came and went quickly, a collective blur to these women. But I stayed, lingered in the halls of their work, which meant they had to see me. I didn't know if that made them uncomfortable.

And still we waited.

In the mornings, not long after dawn, Sam and I would stroll past Sun, our dozing doorman, and across the street into the patio area of a night club where no one arrived before noon. Until then it was our playground. There was a fountain with dried leaves in its centre and a sitting area with a paint-chipped bench. There were makeshift brooms made out of wood and twine that lay like sleeping guards against a wall. Sam picked these up and dragged them around, the handles taller than him. He spied all kinds of bugs that were drawn to light in the dark but curled up to sleep in the day. He pointed at spiders stretched out in their webs, as still as sea stars sunning on a sandbar. Did they think themselves invisible, if they did not move? It was true that their lack of movement meant Sam's interest waned and he moved on in search of other creatures.

The other two Quebec families arrived to pick up their sons. Muriel's husband, Gilbert, arrived alone, and I hugged him tightly. I was so happy to see him and to meet his little boy, Emile. Muriel and I continued our email correspondence, forging something that would last our lifetimes. I think we both knew we were building a family. One where our boys could grow up together with a shared and precious connection. We met so far from home, yet our houses in Montreal were just ten minutes apart. I cried when Gilbert and Emile left. My chest was heavy with envy.

I took Sam into my arms, kissed his face and smelled his skin to remind me that we were blessed. There was a silver lining to being trapped in Seoul for, now that I knew the intensity of those first days, I could not imagine getting on a plane so soon after taking custody. How excruciating those long hours home would have been.

The circumstances that had been forced upon us had provided a cushion of familiarity for my child, hearing a language that wasn't foreign, smelling and eating food he was used to. He didn't have to negotiate so much powerful change all at once. This precious time had allowed Sam to discover for himself, in a place that still felt like home, that it was me he searched for when uncertainty crept too close. That it was my body he leaned into as he fell asleep. He was my baby, and through those long weeks when I wasn't sure how or when or if we would be able to leave, we had found each other, and I would never, ever, let go.

And still we waited.

39 Far From Home

"I'm glad you're still awake." It was Kyunghwa. It was almost midnight and I was shocked to get her call. "I'm coming to pick you up," she said. In her voice was something I could not detect. It was now almost two months since I landed back in Seoul.

"Now?" I asked, "Where are we going?"

"Yes, now. We are going for help."

She was at my door in minutes. Sam was sound asleep, already strapped into the baby carrier on my chest. As we walked down into the night, she explained that a delegation from our home province of Quebec, including the head of the Quebec International Adoption Agency, had just landed in Seoul. The purpose of their visit was to witness the adoption program in South Korea, meet the people who ran it, and visit a few orphanages.

"None of that is going to happen," assured Kyunghwa, "until they meet you and Sam, and figure out how to get you both home."

I clung to her optimism, even though my own had grown threadbare.

"They will help us," she said. "I am sure of it."

"What do you think they will be able to do?" I asked her.

"I don't know. But they must have more power than we do. They must be able to get us answers."

"It's just so strange," I said. "Why would he be the only one lost in the system? It just doesn't make any sense."

"I agree. We ask ourselves the same question every day, Tarah. There is an answer somewhere, though, and the next path to finding it is this one. Now," she said. "We will walk."

I had rarely been out so late at night and I found the energy enchanting. Street lamps switch on, creating a chorus line of moons. There is a restlessness to the silky summer air. Laughter blows out from restaurants, landing as lightly as soap bubbles on bare shoulders before lifting off again.

"What did they say when you explained our situation?" I asked her as we walked.

"They told me to come and meet them," she said. "Their plane landed an hour ago. I did my best to communicate how serious this is, and I think they understood."

As a ceaseless stream of cars zipped by, we walked past outdoor food stalls where the smells of rubber, seafood, and cooking oil had become familiar and comforting. It was wonderful to have Kyunghwa to walk with and to hear Seoul described through her eyes.

"It never stops moving, Tarah. Pushing and pulling from morning to night."

I adored the city, all of its motion and every bit of its fitful energy. Tall buildings loomed before us with giant sliding glass doors that slid open and closed like blades. Kyunghwa stopped suddenly. "We're here," she said.

The hotel lobby was bright and loud. Doormen in caps and fitted uniforms pulled trolleys of luggage, while a reception team handed out keys and ushered travellers down hallways. Well-dressed couples with sleek hair sipped cocktails at the bar. Women spilled out from crowded elevators with printed scarves draped around their necks like waterfalls. I was wearing shorts and a T-shirt, my hair pulled up in a bun, and a sleeping baby in my arms. Kyunghwa and I exchanged a glance, knowing how out of place we were.

"Let's stand over there," she said. "I'll call to let them know we've arrived."

We settled into one of the cushioned couches. Kyunghwa was quiet and shy by nature, but she was very easy to talk to, and I enjoyed her company. It was clear she worked long days; it was almost one o'clock in the morning, and no doubt she would be back in the office first thing.

"Is your home city like this?" she asked me.

"Montreal is very vibrant as well," I told her. "It's charming, with old stone buildings and dramatic architecture. It's not as big or as populous as Seoul, but it has an excitement about it."

"It is very far away," she said.

"Yes, it is," I said, "very far from here."

The Quebec delegation was easy to spot: three women in wrinkled clothes, their shoulders hunched forward as if bringing them that much closer to the beds they craved. They had been travelling all day and must have been exhausted.

"Hello," I said. "Thank you for meeting us so late, I know you've had a long trip."

The head of Quebec's adoption agency was a tall woman with short blonde hair. She was wearing a tailored grey pin-striped suit.

"Help us to understand the problem," said Ms. Vincent, with no pleasantries or introduction. "Why is there no visa?"

We explained what we knew. Every question they asked, we answered, and in the end they were as confused as we were as to why Sam's Canadian visa was denied. They had never encountered a case like this, and they promised to work with us to resolve it as quickly as possible.

"Let me make a call," she said. "We'll start there."

It was morning in Montreal. Ms. Vincent pulled out her cell phone and punched in a number. She explained our case to her assistant, and asked him to contact the authorities in Ottawa.

"Find out what went wrong," she said, "and contact the embassy in Manila. I want to know why there's no visa."

It seemed so easy, a few steps, a couple of phone calls, but since nothing so far had been easy, I didn't expect this would be either. We shook hands, and I wished them a good night.

"Try to sleep, Tarah," Kyunghwa said when she dropped me off at the guest house.

"You too." I took her hand in mine. "Thank you for everything."

"No thanks are needed," she said. "My job is to make sure you leave together and start your life in Canada."

A ringing phone pulled me from my bed early the next morning.

"You should come to the office." Kyunghwa was already there despite the early hour.

"I'm on my way. Is it good news or bad news?"

"It's neither. Come, now."

The news from Canada was that there was no news. No one could explain why we had become lost in the system, or which path would lead us out. The Canadian embassy claimed to have no record of our child—can you believe that? no record!—despite the piles of paperwork I had from them in my possession. As a result, the embassy in Manila, the only place where Sam's visa could be processed, continued to deny us the one document we needed to leave.

A second email had arrived during the night. "This child is not in our system," they wrote again. "No visa will be issued."

"I'm scared," I whispered to Kyunghwa. Sam was hanging in the baby carrier. "What do we do?"

For the first time she had no reassuring words. "Let's give this delegation a chance to find answers," was the most she could offer.

It was impossible not to feel utterly defeated and trapped. There was no trail of breadcrumbs we could follow to get home. Who knew how far into the unknown we were, and how long it was going to take for someone to find us and point us toward the shore.

"We believe the best solution would be to reapply for your child's visa."

"Reapply?" I almost shouted. I wanted to yell. "A visa application takes months, and what if it's refused? No. There has to be another way."

No goddamn way! Find his fucking visa. This is too risky.

"I understand your hesitation," said Ms. Vincent.

"No," I said. "I don't think you do. You have nothing to lose. I have everything to lose. There must be another way. You have to be able to find his visa. There is a mountain of paperwork right here!"

"I'm afraid this is your best option," she said, with zero emotion. "If the embassy won't issue your child a visa, he isn't leaving. It's that simple. If we reapply you will get a new one. We will stay on top of your file and make sure it is fast-tracked."

"What if it's not?" I asked. "What if the visa takes months, or doesn't get approved at all? Plus, aren't you leaving in a few days? Where will that leave us once you're gone?"

She said, "You'll just have to trust me."

She was right, of course, I had no other option.

We spent the next two hours filling out more than a dozen documents, making copies, signing papers, attaching translations, and when it was finally sent off, I was told what I had been told so often during this endless process. Wait. Just wait, Tarah. Wait and have faith.

As the last of the papers hissed through the scanner, I slumped into the couches of the adoption office. Then I pulled myself up and placed my feet flat on the floor. I looked at my child, took a deep breath and slowly exhaled. In that moment I understood with grace and humility how profoundly the decision to stay in Asia had changed Enrico's and my life together. If I had gone back to Canada without Sam, the confusion and ever-present complications surrounding his file would have been dealt with far more slowly, if at all. There would have been no urgency to fix it. He would have continued to grow in the arms of his foster family while Enrico and I remained far away, burning for answers that would not come.

The delegation from Canada left two days later.

"You will hear from us soon, Ms. Schwartz," said Ms. Vincent.

"Please," I begged. "Please, don't forget about us."

There was nothing sentimental in her answer. She simply said, "I won't." I had absolutely no other choice but to believe her.

40 Forgiveness

"I'm sure this is the reason," said Enrico, nervous and anxious all at once. "It's the only thing that makes sense."

It was Enrico who finally figured it out.

"I've gone over all of our documents," he continued, "and our first adoption is the only variable. It's the only thing that sets our file apart. The problem has got to revolve around the adoption that didn't work out."

He had spent untold hours on the phone, too many of them on hold, had had numerous talks with embassy workers and officials, had spent an obscene amount of his days thinking about our case, and had challenged every person he could to help him understand what went wrong.

"Tell them to look into that," he said. "I'm sure of it."

He was right.

Several days after the Quebec delegation left Seoul, Kyunghwa knocked at my door. It was late, and I was surprised to see her as she hadn't called to let me know she was coming. Kyunghwa's mood was strange, fitful stories skipped across her eyes, as if they did not know which turn or curve would settle them. She was distracted, weighed down by something that made her appear tired. We sat together, her hands clenched so tightly in her lap they shone white.

"What's wrong?" I asked her. "Is it about the visa?"

"Yes and no," she answered.

"What do you mean?"

"Your husband was right. The problem was the first adoption," she said. "But there is more."

I remained still, unsure how bad that "more" was going to get.

"It is our fault, Tarah," she said. "The visa did not come, has not come, because of us."

"I don't understand," I said.

"Because your first adoption had been finalized," she continued, unable to look up from the floor, "a visa had already been issued by Canada for that child. We never sent it back—we did not know we needed to."

With that visa tucked into a drawer somewhere in Seoul, never cancelled or returned, according to the embassy records, our file was quite simply closed. The return of those initial documents would have signalled a cancelled adoption, and Sam's file would have been opened in its place. His visa would have been issued, without obstacle or complication, with the other Quebec children. Kyunghwa told me all this quietly.

"We are so sorry, Tarah."

She did not have to tell me. The blame could have stayed buried between our two worlds, under layers of sand and silt, but Kyunghwa was a woman of honour. It was important that I be made aware so that an apology could be offered and forgiveness requested. There was no need for either, I told her.

"You and your team have been nothing but wonderful to me," I said. "You gave me the greatest gift of my life. You gave me Sam. Nothing else matters."

We cannot choose the roads we are sent down, only how we react once we are on them. There had been incredible gifts on this path. I had met extraordinary women, created a bond with my baby, and lived in a culture different from my own, halfway around the world.

"There is nothing to apologize for," I said. "I am blessed to know you. I am grateful."

But Kyunghwa needed forgiveness, so I gave it to her. She touched her forehead to mine—a gesture filled with such tenderness it felt warm to the touch.

The delegation had kept their promise. They hadn't forgotten about us. As we finally found out what had gone wrong, something went very right.

Sam's visa arrived the next day.

41 Endings

They threw us a party.

Sam and I stepped off the elevator one final time, walked down the toy- and-stroller-strewn hallway, and bounded happily through the doors of the adoption office to the chorus of "Hel-lo Sam!"

"Here it is," said Kyungwha, walking quickly toward me. "Finally."

She placed a large manilla envelope, marked urgent, into my hands. It was Sam's visa. The entire room stood and started clapping.

"Thank you," I said, full of emotion. "I'm very grateful to you all."

Balloons hung from the ceiling, and ribbons dripped down from them. A table was laden with a tower of yellow bananas, sweets of all kinds, sandwiches, and crispy Korean snacks.

"Come and sit," they squealed, pulling me toward the table. "It is for you."

The entire office had been invited, from case workers to accountants. For several hours we laughed, ate, and let Sam entertain us. Hyeyoung pulled Sam into her lap for a final caress and motherly wishes for a full and happy life. She had watched him grow, had been there since the beginning, had been by our side through it all.

"This is for you." I gave her a silver bracelet surrounded by hearts. "For all the love."

Hyeyoung bowed her head. "I will not forget either of you," she whispered.

Kyunghwa presented me with a Korean box inlaid with mother of pearl.

"A gift from us all, Tarah," she said. "Most children leave so quickly once the parents come. It has been our great pleasure to witness the bond grow between mother and child. That is the gift you leave us."

"*Kamsahamnida*," I said. "Thank you. Thank you for my son."

Those final days in Seoul were filled with a rare beauty. I became acutely aware of endings. Relationships that had been cultivated with such care would fade, like flowers, once we left. There was too much distance and too many differences to expect more. *It was exactly what it was meant to be,* I thought. People touch one another's lives, however briefly. Then, as hard as it feels, we say, "*Thank you, I will remember you.*" We hold them close and then we let them go.

42 Behind the Doors of the Third Floor

"I can't believe it's finally over," Enrico said. "You've been gone so long."

"We'll be home soon," I told him. "Our plane leaves very early in the morning, so I better get some sleep."

"Do you have everything you need?" he asked. "It's going to be a long trip."

"We'll be OK," I assured him. "I'll see you at the airport. I'll be the one with the baby."

"I love you," he said. "Travel safe."

My one suitcase was like a giant avocado, overly ripe, and ready to burst. Laying my body's weight on it, I coaxed the zipper's last teeth to clamp shut, and counted on it holding together for the trip home.

Then I heard a horrible thud. When I turned around, Sam's face was covered in blood.

He had lost his footing and hit his mouth on the sharp wood corner of the bed frame. I had never seen how quickly lips can bleed, but within seconds his chin was dripping with blood. He began wailing, his eyes wide and round as saucers.

It took me two giant steps. I pulled him into my arms, grabbed a dish towel from the kitchen and ran out of our room. Holding the cloth to his lips I headed for the stairs, and, in my bare feet, tore down two flights to face the double doors of the third floor. In the black of night, the doors seemed larger, with more locks than I had noticed before. A dozen sets of slippers were placed neatly by the wall, so many pairs tucked side by side.

The cloth at Sam's mouth was red and wet with blood and tears. I banged my fist on the doors. When they opened, a woman dressed head to toe in pink looked at me with questioning eyes. There I was in an oversized T-shirt, no pants or shoes, and a bleeding baby in my arms. I must have been quite a sight.

"Can you help me?" I asked. "Please."

Barely dressed and frantic, I took my first steps across the mysterious frontier.

She led me to an office that contained one desk and one chair where several women bustled in and out to tend to Sam. They were talking so fast, but I could only stare at them and shake my head. I didn't understand what they were saying. I was scared and alone. They tried to see how badly he was cut, but he was crying, clinging to me, refusing to show his face, the blood from his lip seeping through the cloth, down my neck and soaking into my shirt.

That's when a young woman approached us and stared affectionately at Sam.

"Geon," she said.

Sam turned his head toward her, and I saw his watery eyes ripple with some faraway feeling. She knelt down and said the name again.

It was Sam's Korean name. Dressed head to toe in lilac scrubs, she pointed at Sam. She then placed her arms as if she was cradling a sleeping baby. Then she pointed to herself.

I understood that this young woman had been one of the many women who had cared for my son before I could care for him myself. She gently stroked his arm, remembering.

Still at work, Hyeyoung and Kyunghwa arrived within minutes. I was so grateful to see them both. Hyeyoung pushed the hair from my face and coaxed Sam into her arms. His lip was cut and swollen but the bleeding had finally stopped.

This was the situation that finally led me to see what was behind the double doors of the third floor. It was like having the breath pulled from my body, torn out and held just beyond my reach. My eyes, so surprised by what they saw, refused to blink or turn away. My feet stayed stuck to the ground, glued there by shock that travelled down my legs like lightning bolts.

The floor was a maternity ward. There were rows and rows and rows of bassinets lined up side by side, filling two giant rooms separated by a long wooden partition. Inside each basket was a baby, many of them whimpering. I must have been so caught up in what was happening with Sam that I hadn't heard anything but him. Now, I heard the cries of a hundred babies. Maybe more.

Half the room was filled with tiny newborns in baskets. So tiny, their legs and arms were covered with the crinkled skin of brand-new lives, pulling at the air for arms they desperately wanted to reach back.

On the other side of the room were more rows and more bassinets. Older babies, maybe four to eight-month-olds, were sitting up, some with wide eyes stunned into silence, others wailing for someone to pluck them from their beds and hold them close. Walking through the rows, tending to each baby in turn, were the women in the pastel uniforms I had seen so often over the last months. There were at least a dozen of them, dressed like gumdrops, roaming the isles with soft hands and sympathetic eyes, smelling of diapers, lavender laundry soap, and baby powder. Some soothed crying babies, slipping milky bottles through eager lips, while others cleaned dirty bottoms or wiped sweat-covered brows that smelled of sorrow. It would have been impossible to give all these children what they wanted more than anything:

fathomless comfort. There were just too many of them. And in the air, which swelled with sadness and pulsed with need and urgency, there was no escaping the heartache that hung over it all. Like a trapped cloud, there was no place for the heartache to go. This was where my baby had begun his life, and it was where so many other children were beginning theirs.

I pulled Sam back into my arms and thanked God so fiercely in that moment. That from these rows and rows of babies, all aching to be cherished, from those endless beds filled with frightened, fragile souls, my son had been chosen for us. With him curled against me, I took the hand of the woman in pastel purple who had recognized Sam, and squeezed it.

"*Kamsahamnida*," I said, overcome with gratitude.

The young woman smiled then walked back toward the cries that pulled at her like magnets. She would remember them all. These children, all of them, were valued. Just before I turned to leave, I saw her pick up a baby girl and hold her to her heart.

The third floor's double doors shut behind us as we left. The mystery, now revealed, still burned behind my eyes, so I closed them, hoping to let the image go, though I knew I would never forget it.

Hyeyoung and Kyunghwa walked us back up to the fifth floor.

"Thank you," I said. "For coming. It was very kind of you."

"We are here for you, Tarah, and for Sam," said Kyunghwa.

"I will miss you very much," I told them. "Nothing, nothing would have been the same without you."

"Live a happy life," she said. "That is what we want for you both."

"I promise we will come back and visit one day," I said. "It may take us a while but, I promise, we will come back."

"It will bring us great pleasure to see you again, whenever that may be."

I hugged them, filled with the burden that departures can bring.

"*Annyeong*, my friends," I said. Goodbye.

"*Annyeong*," they both said. I looked into Kyunghwa's eyes, one blue and one brown, and saw that she was crying.

43 Back Around the World

I woke while the city was still sleeping. Slipping away from Sam still curled on the bed, I sat near the window and stared at an inky sky dotted with faraway clouds. It was silent outside our room. I imagined our old doorman Sun dozing downstairs, his neck tilted, his breathing slow and rhythmic, guarding all the babies asleep on the third floor.

The bright pink tiles of the bar across the street flashed in the moonlight. The shadows cast by tall, wide street-lamps stretched out on the sidewalk. A mountain rose up in the distance. I had never seen the city so quiet and undisturbed.

I was going to miss Seoul: the sounds, the smells, the language, the people. But it was time to go. Stepping over to the bed, I rubbed Sam's silky skin. "It's time to go, my baby. Wake up, we're going home."

Sun arrived, sleepy-eyed and smelling of stale coffee, to help carry down our suitcase. We paused in the darkness, now growing thinner with the approach of morning, and stood on the steps outside the building. It's where we had sat together on many wistful evenings watching the city lose its sharp lines and rough edges.

"Goodbye," he said, bowing.

"*Annyeonghi gyeseyo*," I replied, which in formal Korean is a farewell that translates into *stay well*.

He then said something to Sam in Korean. I don't know what his parting words were. I wish I did know. Somehow, though, I feel certain they were blessings for a full life. He touched Sam's cheek with hands that looked like well-worn leather. He then turned and walked back into the guest house.

I watched him until he slumped down behind his desk. He raised his hand to wave at us. I waved back.

Once we arrived at Incheon Airport, I was eager to board and take off. I wasn't going to feel completely safe or at ease until we had left the country. A nagging feeling lingered, pressing on insecurity and doubt. *We're not out yet*, I kept thinking. I watched as a specialized agent leafed through each of our documents at the ticket counter. Infuriatingly, painstakingly, slow with no expression on her face, she examined each of our papers multiple times. Every few moments she stopped to glance up at Sam, who was strapped to my chest but wide awake. She never once looked at me. She didn't ask me a single question. My body temperature was rising, and my hands grew damp with sweat. I issued yet another silent prayer that everything was in order, that every document needed was there.

Please, please let this be over.

The tick tock of the airport clocks was too loud, the breathing of people in line behind me sounded like waves, feet shuffled, bags scraped, intercoms called, hands ran through hair, zippers zipped, electronic doors swept open and closed. Tick tock. Still no word, no questions. It was interminable. Then her hand moved and pulled from under her desk a large silver stamp pad. I watched her open it, curl her fingers around the handle of the pad, and then, as though in slow motion, her hand came down, slamming with a giant, satisfying thud over and over again onto each of our papers.

"You can go," she said. "You can both go."

We were through.

I pulled the seatbelt around us both, locking us into our seat. Sam's hands curled around mine as he stared out at the tarmac. He looked up at me, wondering. I did what I had been doing for weeks. I explained, in a language that he did not understand, that we were going home, that he was safe. I kissed the top of his head and told him I was there. I would always be there.

Even as the plane lined up for its turn to take off, the tiniest fear reared and scratched at my insides. We were still on Korean soil, and because of that, I did not feel far enough away to be certain that no one could take him from me. Finally, the plane taxied, lifted off, ascended, and after six long years of wanting to be a mother, of living through heartache and heartbreak, of getting up, falling down, and pulling myself back together again, I exhaled.

He was mine. Sam was my baby. As the plane flew higher, on its way back around the world, I finally felt that no one and nothing could change that.

44 The Offering

We landed in Montreal after almost twenty-four hours of travel.

"Welcome to Canada, little man!"

Our immigration officer was incredibly cheerful. He stamped Sam's documents, handed them back to me and said, "Congratulations, he's special."

I smiled. "Yes. Yes, he is. Thank you."

And there, just beyond the glass doors, was my beaming husband. He ran to us and pulled us into his arms.

"I'm so happy you're both home," he said. "I never want to be separated like that again."

"We won't be, I promise. We're home now."

He took Sam's hand in his. I smiled, knowing that they were about to embark on the extraordinary journey of becoming father and son. So new to each other, they would find a special place in the world for just the two of them. And it would be beautiful.

Sam fell asleep dangling at my chest. Enrico snapped a picture of us. One long journey had come to an end. We were parents now, and so much lay before us. The long road to get here had taken much away, left holes the size of fists in places sore and fragile, but those spaces were filling up now. The smell of Sam's skin, the sound of his voice, his touch—it was a balm. All the twists and turns we'd taken, some by choice and others not, had led us here. To Sam.

Curled in each other's arms that first night back, Enrico whispered of all the moments that were to come.

"I can't believe he's ours," he said. "Our baby."

"He's a gift," I whispered back. "It was all worth it. All of it."

There existed a crystalline understanding of what it had taken to get to this moment and this place.

As Enrico slept, I tiptoed back to Sam, incapable of staying away from him for too long. He looked so serene, and as I stood there, he woke and reached for me. I took him into my arms, as I had done every night since becoming his mother, and held him close. As I stared into his eyes, I saw a kind of peace offering from the universe.

"Will this do?" it asked.

I nodded, and kissed each of Sam's silky eyelids.

"Oh, yes," I said. "This will do."

EPILOGUE

So much has happened since that long journey from Seoul. Every moment of it I treasure and keep safe in my heart.

Arriving in Montreal was yet another huge transition for Sam. He was only eighteen months old, and a new city with a new home brought more immense changes. But our darling boy has a happy nature, and once again he showed how strong and brave he is. He also had something else to hold onto during that difficult shift, something familiar. This time he had me.

We rarely left our home that first month back, keeping eager family members at bay and working on solidifying the attachment between my husband, myself, and our son. After cocooning, attachment is the next important step in the life of adopted children. It's crucial to the bonding process. Time alone is what makes that bond possible. And in many ways, it's priceless.

This was when we discovered how often Sam makes us laugh. And how he gently pats your back, when you hold him in your arms. This was also when he said "Mama" clearly for the first time. When he truly felt it and was finally able to say it. It's when we became a family, when we realized there is nothing we wouldn't do for him.

Friends encouraged me to write it all down. To tell our story. It has taken me years to realize that perhaps our journey can give people what I desperately needed for so long: hope.

Peter once wrote, "It's not important that you never lose hope, it's important that you find it again."

I had found it again. I also think I needed an ending. Caught up in grief, I hadn't been able to find the strength to put into words what sorrow can do to someone. How it ages you. How sorrow, when it finds you, turns the shell of who you are into something tender and pale. The danger is that you will spill out and remain empty forever.

"It's important in life to have people who know our story," Peter said. He told me writing it down would allow me to travel through my life with less on my shoulders. I believe that is true. I still have not met Peter in person. He has seen many pictures of Sam and writes regularly to check in. He reminds me to tug at the cosmos if I ever need him, or simply to share the special moments.

"In the process of helping you try to make sense of the impossible," Peter wrote, "you made me feel valuable and relevant, and that was an important stepping stone back to life. It feels good inside my broken parts to have helped you."

I became pregnant a few months after returning from Korea. A baby had begun life inside my body. But it did not stay: I miscarried after three months. Holding myself through intimate hurts, I watched another potential life spill away. As I faced that horrible hurt once again, I learned something I had not known before. That my heart—all hearts—have great power. They are capable of keeping within them immense joy as well as pain.

Sam helped me heal. Adoption is a labour of the soul. You take a great breath and then exhale minute by minute, day by day, year after year, until a tiny precious being is placed in your hands asking to be cherished. Our son has given us more than I can ever possibly put into words. When I feel him pressed against me, there is simply nowhere else in the world I would rather be. When I tuck him in at night, and he places his palm on my cheek, I stare at him, refusing to blink because I don't want to miss a single second.

"I love you Mama," he says as he touches my face. Not because I said it first, or because I prompted him, but because he really and truly feels it. He hugs me and smiles that glorious smile of his, which takes up his entire face, and then he falls asleep. I can spend endless hours watching as his breathing slows and he relaxes into dreams. He's so angelic, so perfect.

With all that Sam has lived in his short life, I am in awe of his strength. He inspires me to be better in every possible way. His life reminds me not to be afraid. I know that every step it has taken to get here, all those years of waiting, every heartbreak and disappointment, every piece of me that had been broken and put back together, has been worth it.

When the idea of motherhood had begun to fade in me, it forced me to ask questions of myself, forced me to choose between giving up and fighting on, between fear and faith, between doubt and belief. In the end, we persevered and found that time and love can heal. Even with my sweet baby by my side, my scars remain. It has taken me so long to accept who I have become through it all. But I have done that. I am comfortable with my scars now. They don't frighten me anymore, because they are not all I see.

Over the years, many women in situations similar to mine have approached me looking for hope, for understanding, for any kindness I can offer. They need a hand to hold, someone who knows the sorrow and heartbreak of infertility. Because sometimes even those who cherish you most can't soothe away the hurt if they haven't felt it themselves. I listen as honestly as I can, and whisper the words that helped me when I was so low my breath made shadows on the pavement.

You will survive this.
You will fall.
You will get up

You will change.
You will hurt.
You will weep.
You will know sorrow.
You will find acceptance.
You will cultivate compassion.
You will heal.

From the most gut-wrenching hurt, from loss, from pain, from grief—you will heal.

How we heal is personal. It does not matter what name we attribute to our beliefs: God, Faith, Hope. It is whatever helps us find light in the dark. How we heal is what inspires, changes, challenges us to be brave. It is what encourages, embraces, and touches us. How we heal is what makes beauty easy to see when it still hurts to look, it is what helps to cultivate grace and kindness.

Find what it is that helps you heal, then hang on for dear life.

Acknowledgements

My deepest thanks to publisher Linda Leith as well as associate publisher Leila Marshy. Without these extraordinary women, this book would never have bloomed. They pushed me to be more honest, more open, more vulnerable and more concise. I will be forever grateful for their guidance and trust.

My thanks as well to early readers who not only provided their insights, but their assurances that I had something worth sharing. They include: Lori Graham, Maya Johnson, Angela MacKenzie and Karen Caouette. Thanks to Deanna Radford for her valuable observations and Pascale Drevillon for sensitivity reading.

To my family for their love and support: my mother Elizabeth, father Eli (I miss you), mother-in-law Odette, sister Aileen, brother Warren, brother-in-law Farooq and nieces Sarah and Kalilah, as well as a wide and wonderful group from Quebec to Ireland to Israel.

Finally, to my life partner and best friend, Enrico. Thank you for giving me the time to heal, to write and to tell our story. You are my rock. And to Sam, my darling boy, my sunshine. Being your mama is the greatest joy of my life. You are my heart.

Tarah Schwartz
Montreal